Dickinson

Structure and Speaking Practice

Third Edition

www.els.edu

Taken from:

Fundamentals of English Grammar, Fourth Edition with Answer Key
by Betty S. Azar and Stacy A. Hagen

Top Notch: English for Today's World 2, Second Edition
by Joan Saslow and Allen Ascher

Top Notch: English for Today's World 3, Second Edition
by Joan Saslow and Allen Ascher

NorthStar: Listening and Speaking Level 3, Third Edition
by Helen S. Solórzano and Jennifer P. L. Schmidt

Fundamentals of English Grammar, Fourth Edition Workbook
by Betty S. Azar, Rachel Spack Koch, and Stacy A. Hagen

Understanding and Using English Grammar, Fourth Edition
by Betty S. Azar and Stacy A. Hagen

Top Notch: English for Today's World 2, Second Edition Workbook
by Joan Saslow and Allen Ascher

Understanding and Using English Grammar, Fourth Edition Workbook
by Betty S. Azar and Stacy A. Hagen

Basic English Grammar, Third Edition Workbook
by Betty Schrampfer Azar and Stacy A. Hagen

Basic English Grammar, Third Edition with Answer Key
by Betty Schrampfer Azar and Stacy A. Hagen

Focus on Grammar 4: An Integrated Skills Approach, Third Edition
by Marjorie Fuchs and Margaret Bonner

Top Notch: English for Today's World 3, Second Edition Workbook
by Joan Saslow and Allen Ascher

Fundamentals of English Grammar, Fourth Edition
by Betty S. Azar and Stacy A. Hagen

Focus on Grammar 3: An Integrated Skills Approach, Fourth Edition
by Marjorie Fuchs, Margaret Bonner, and Miriam Westheimer

Cover image courtesy of kemie/iStockphoto.

Development Project Manager: Courtney Towson
Production Project Manager: Liz Faerm
Photo Editor: Jamie Wilson
Associate Acquisitions Editor: Pamela Vitu

Taken from:

Fundamentals of English Grammar,
 Fourth Edition with Answer Key
by Betty S. Azar and Stacy A. Hagen
Copyright © 2011, 2003, 1992, 1985
 by Betty Schrampfer Azar
Published by Pearson Longman
White Plains, New York 10606

Top Notch: English for Today's World 2,
 Second Edition
by Joan Saslow and Allen Ascher
Copyright © 2011 by Pearson
 Education, Inc.
Published by Pearson Longman

Top Notch: English for Today's World 3,
 Second Edition
by Joan Saslow and Allen Ascher
Copyright © 2011 by Pearson
 Education, Inc.
Published by Pearson Longman

*NorthStar: Listening and Speaking
 Level 3,* Third Edition
by Helen S. Solórzano and Jennifer
 P. L. Schmidt
Copyright © 2009, 2004, 1998 by
 Pearson Education, Inc.
Published by Pearson Longman

Fundamentals of English Grammar,
 Fourth Edition Workbook
by Betty S. Azar, Rachel Spack Koch,
 and Stacy A. Hagen
Copyright © 2011, 2003, 1992, 1985
 by Betty Schrampfer Azar
Published by Pearson Longman

*Understanding and Using English
 Grammar,* Fourth Edition
by Betty S. Azar and Stacy A. Hagen
Copyright © 2009, 2002, 1989, 1981
 by Betty Schrampfer Azar
Published by Pearson Longman

Top Notch: English for Today's World 2,
 Second Edition Workbook
by Joan Saslow and Allen Ascher
Copyright © 2011 by Pearson
 Education, Inc.
Published by Pearson Longman

*Understanding and Using English
 Grammar,* Fourth Edition Workbook
by Betty S. Azar and Stacy A. Hagen
Copyright © 2009, 2000, 1992 by
 Pearson Education, Inc.
Published by Pearson Longman

Basic English Grammar, Third Edition
 Workbook
by Betty Schrampfer Azar and Stacy A.
 Hagen
Copyright © 2006 by Betty Schrampfer
 Azar
Published by Longman

Basic English Grammar, Third Edition
 with Answer Key
by Betty Schrampfer Azar and Stacy A.
 Hagen
Copyright © 2006, 1996, 1984 by
 Betty Schrampfer Azar
Published by Longman

*Focus on Grammar 4: An Integrated
 Skills Approach,* Third Edition
by Marjorie Fuchs and Margaret Bonner
Copyright © 2006, 2000, 1995 by
 Pearson Education, Inc.
Published by Pearson Longman

Top Notch: English for Today's World 3,
 Second Edition Workbook
by Joan Saslow and Allen Ascher
Copyright © 2011 by Pearson
 Education, Inc.
Published by Pearson Longman

Fundamentals of English Grammar,
 Fourth Edition
by Betty S. Azar and Stacy A. Hagen
Copyright © 2011, 2003, 1992, 1985
 by Betty Schrampfer Azar
Published by Pearson Longman

*Focus on Grammar 3: An Integrated
 Skills Approach,* Fourth Edition
by Marjorie Fuchs, Margaret Bonner,
 and Miriam Westheimer
Copyright © 2011, 2006, 2000, 1994
 by Pearson Education, Inc.
Published by Pearson Longman

All trademarks, service marks, registered trademarks, and
registered service marks are the property of their respective
owners and are used herein for identification purposes only.

Pearson Learning Solutions, 501 Boylston Street, Suite 900,
Boston, MA 02116
A Pearson Education Company
www.pearsoned.com

Printed in the United States of America

13   17

000200010271269797

CT/JW

ISBN 10: 1-256-64967-8
ISBN 13: 978-1-256-64967-0

CONTENTS

UNIT 4

Health Matters 51

UNIT 5

About Personality 71

UNIT 6

Culture and Commerce 93

APPENDIX 1

APPENDIX 2

LEARNING OBJECTIVES

Unit	Communication Goals	Vocabulary	Grammar	Conversation Strategies	Listening/ Pronunciation
1 Getting Things Done page 1	• Convincing others • Requesting service	• Helping others • Services	• Passive • Causatives • Passive causatives	• Expressing urgency	**Listening tasks:** • Placing orders • Asking for a favor • Offering help
2 Eating Well page 17	• Talking about likes and dislikes • Discussing past habits	• Diet • Food groups	• Past habit • *Used to/would* • *Be used to/ accustomed to* • *Get used to/ accustomed to* • *Another/the other* • *Other(s)/the other(s)*	• Talking about choices • Accepting and rejecting offers	**Listening task:** • Food passions **Pronunciation:** • Reducing used to
3 Living with Computers page 37	• Troubleshoot problems • Recommend a better deal • Describe how you use computers • Discuss the impact of the internet	• Computer terms • The internet • Comparative adjectives	• Comparisons with as • Comparisons with *less . . . than* and *not as . . . as* • Modifying comparatives	• Asking for help	**Listening task:** • Recommendation **Pronunciation:** • Stress in as . . . as phrases
4 Health Matters page 51	• Calling in sick • Make a medical or dental appointment • Talk about medications	• Aches • Pains • Illnesses • Medications	• Modal auxiliaries	• Describing ailments • Expressing possibility and ability • Expressing logical conclusions	**Listening task:** • Conversations with doctors **Pronunciation:** • Intonation of lists
5 About Personality page 71	• Getting to know what someone likes • Cheer someone up	• Positive and negative adjectives	• Gerunds and infinitives • Gerunds as objects of prepositions • Gerunds and infinitives as direct objectives • Gerunds as subjects	• Giving advice • Making suggestions • Expressing opinions • Discussing plans	**Listening task:** • Discussing home decor **Pronunciation:** • Reduction of to in infinitives

Unit	Communication Goals	Vocabulary	Grammar	Conversation Strategies	Listening/ Pronunciation
6 Culture and Commerce page 93	• Discuss the relationship between culture and commerce • Make predictions about the future • Expressing agreement and disagreement	• Tourism	• Real conditionals	• Discuss the positive or negative effects of something • Future predictions	**Listening tasks:** • For main ideas, details, inferences • Making inferences about people's feelings
Appendices page 107			• Causative verbs • Expressing past habits • Comparison: as . . . as • Expressing ability and possibility • Polite Questions • Preposition + Gerund • If Clauses • Important words and phrases		

ABOVE MATERIAL FROM: ELS LANGUAGE CENTERS

ACKNOWLEDGMENTS

The Third Edition of our ELS SSP and Reading & Writing texts is the culmination of nearly two-and-a-half years of hard work by countless individuals from ELS Language Centers in the US, Canada, and Australia. This project began in the winter of 2011 when we convened our Curriculum Revision Committee. The fourteen teachers, Academic Directors, and Center Directors who sat on this committee and saw the process through from start to finish are deserving of individual recognition for their tireless work: Lesley Carroll, Morgan Foster, Raylene Houck, Liz Hurysz, Dan Manolescu, Catherine Mason, Bernadette McGlynn, Mary McKay, Gerardo Mestizo, Scott Myers, Jim Scofield, Marie Silva, Carol Wright, and Lisagail Zeitlin.

This committee used their years of classroom teaching experience, study in curriculum design and ESL methodology, and intimate understanding of our ELS students to complete this tremendous task. The project involved, among other things, reviewing and refining specific language skills objectives for each level and text, reviewing hundreds of ESL texts, creating content, and organizing thematic units following a communicative approach to language instruction. Two sessions of piloting, five rounds of editing, and 27 months later, I am proud to present these texts to our ELS students.

I would also like to thank the 26 ELS centers and their academic teams that volunteered to pilot these texts, and over 50 ELS teachers who provided invaluable feedback. The feedback from teachers who used the texts gave us important insight into the practical use of these texts in the classroom and provided the basis for hundreds of edits and improvements.

A special thanks also to Terri Rapoport, Director of Curriculum Development, Susan Matson, Director of Teacher Training and Development, and Ward Morrow, Director of Academic Affairs, who, in addition to editing the texts, worked closely with our Curriculum Revision Committee and provided guidance, support, and advice.

In addition, we would like to thank Pearson Education, our publishing partner, for their collaborative effort in the preparation of the new edition. We'd also like to add a particular note of thanks to the Pearson Learning Solutions Rights Management group for their work in providing a significant amount of photo research for the series. The new photos help to shape the book and make it a more effective teaching and learning tool in print and digital formats.

Finally, thank you to all our academic staff and students for your belief in the power of teaching and learning English—and helping the world communicate better. May we all contribute to more peace, friendship, and understanding among all peoples of the world.

Mark W. Harris
President and CEO
ELS Educational Services

UNIT 1

Getting Things Done

GOALS By the end of Unit 1, you will be able to:

1 Get someone else to do something.

2 Request express service.

A *Answer the following questions about yourself.*

nǧ trì hoãn, câu giờ.

Are You a PROCRASTINATOR?

Take the survey.

1. At the beginning of every week, you _____.
   - ☐ **a.** always make to-do lists for your calendar *lịch*
   - ☐ **b.** sometimes make to-do lists, but you often forget
   - ☑ **c.** don't bother with planning and just let things happen

2. When you need to buy someone a gift, you _____.
   - ☐ **a.** get something right away
   - ☑ **b.** buy something a few days before you have to give it
   - ☐ **c.** pick something up on the day you have to give it

3. When you have something that's broken, you _____. *bị hỏng*
   - ☐ **a.** immediately take it in to be repaired
   - ☑ **b.** wait for a convenient time to take it in
   - ☐ **c.** never get around to taking it in

4. When you have a lot of things you need to do, you do _____.
   - ☐ **a.** the hardest things first
   - ☐ **b.** the easiest things first
   - ☑ **c.** anything but what you need to do

5. When you need to get something done in a short amount of time, you _____.
- ☐ **a.** feel motivated to work even harder
- ☑ **b.** feel a little nervous, but you get to work
- ☐ **c.** have a hard time doing it

6. You _____ feel bad when there are things you haven't gotten done yet.
- ☐ **a.** always
- ☑ **b.** sometimes
- ☐ **c.** rarely

Your results

If you answered "c" four or more times:
You are a classic procrastinator! You tend to put things off.

If you answered "b" four or more times:
You are a bit of a procrastinator, but you try to get things done on time.

If you answered "a" four or more times:
You are organized and self-motivated. You never put off what you can get done now.

Source: adapted from www.blogthings.com.

B PAIR WORK

Compare responses on the survey with a partner. Does your score accurately describe the kind of person you are? Explain, using examples.

C 🎧 PHOTO STORY

Read and listen to some customers placing orders at a copy shop.

Manager: What can I do for you today, Ms. Krauss?
Customer 1: I need to get these documents copied a.s.a.p.* Think I could get 300 copies done by 11:00?
Manager: I'm afraid that might be difficult. I've got a lot of orders to complete this morning.
Customer 1: Sorry. I know this is last minute. But it's really urgent.
Manager: Well, you're a good customer. Let me see what I can do.
Customer 1: Thanks a million. You're a lifesaver!

*a.s.a.p. = as soon as possible

Answer the following questions.

1. What does the customer need?

2. When does she need this done?

ABOVE MATERIAL FROM: TOP NOTCH 3, SECOND EDITION

3. What does the manager agree to do?

4. Why does he agree to help?

Manager: Excuse me . . . Hello. Happy Copy.
Customer 2: Hi, Sam. Ken Li here.
Manager: Hi, Mr. Li. How can I help you today?
Customer 2: Well, I'm going through my to-do list, and I just realized I need to get fifty 30-page sales binders made up for our meeting next week. Any chance I could get them done by first thing tomorrow morning?
Manager: Tomorrow morning? No sweat. Can you get the documents to me before noon?
Customer 2: Absolutely. I owe you one, Sam!

Answer the following questions.

1. What does the customer need?

2. When does the customer need this done?

3. Can the manager help the customer?

Manager: Sorry to keep you waiting, Ms. Krauss.
Customer 1: Well, I see that you've got a lot on your plate today. I won't keep you any longer.
Manager: Don't worry, Ms. Krauss. We'll get your order done on time.
Customer 1: Should I give you a call later?
Manager: No need for that. Come at 11:00 and I'll have your documents ready.
Customer 1: Thanks, Sam.

Answer the following questions.

1. Is the manager having a busy day or a slow day?

2. Does the customer need her order immediately or can she wait?

3. Will the manager finish her order today or tomorrow?

GRAMMAR

chủ / bị động

ACTIVE SENTENCES AND PASSIVE SENTENCES

Active **a.** The mouse *ate* the cheese. **Passive** **b.** The cheese *was eaten* by the mouse.	Examples (a) and (b) have the same meaning.
Active 	**Passive** 
Active S **c.** *Bob* mailed the package. **Passive** S **d.** The package was mailed *by + O* by *Bob*.	In (c): The object in an active sentence becomes the subject in a passive sentence. In (d): The subject in an active sentence is the object of *by* in a passive sentence.

FORM OF THE PASSIVE

	be + past participle		Form of all passive verbs: *be* + *past participle* *Be* can be in any of its forms: *am, is, are, was, were, has been, have been, will be, etc.*
a. Corn	*is*	*grown* by farmers.	
b. Sara	*was*	*surprised* by the news.	
c. The report	*will be*	*written* by Mary.	

	Active	Passive
SIMPLE PRESENT $H \top \ominus$	Farmers *grow* corn. ⟶	Corn *is grown* by farmers.
SIMPLE PAST $Q \kappa \ominus$	The news *surprised* Sara. ⟶	Sara *was surprised* by the news.
PRESENT PROGRESSIVE $H \top \top D$	Diana *is copying* the letters. ⟶	The letters *are being copied* by Diana.
PAST PROGRESSIVE $Q \kappa \top D$	Diana *was copying* the letters. ⟶	The letters *were being copied* by Diana.
PRESENT PERFECT $H \top H \top$	Jack *has mailed* the letter. ⟶	The letter *has been mailed* by Jack.
FUTURE $7 \text{L} \omega.$	Mr. Lee *will plan* the meeting. ⟶ Sue *is going to write* the report. ⟶	The meeting *will be planned* by Mr. Lee. The report *is going to be written* by Sue.

 ABOVE MATERIAL FROM: FUNDAMENTALS OF ENGLISH GRAMMAR, FOURTH EDITION

A *Change the active verbs to passive by adding the correct form of* **be**. *Include the subject of the passive sentence.*

1. Simple Present

   a. The teacher *helps* **me**.   ____I____ _____am_____ **helped** by the teacher.

   b. The teacher *helps* **Eva**.   ___Eva___ _____is_____ **helped** by the teacher.

   c. The teacher *helps* **us**.   _____ _____ **helped** by the teacher.

2. Simple Past

   a. The teacher *helped* **him**.   _____ _____ **helped** by the teacher.

   b. The teacher *helped* **them**.   _____ _____ **helped** by the teacher.

3. Present Progressive

   a. The teacher *is helping* **us**.   _____ _____ **helped** by the teacher.

   b. The teacher *is helping* **her**.   _____ _____ **helped** by the teacher.

4. Past Progressive

   a. The teacher *was helping* **me**.   _____ _____ **helped** by the teacher.

   b. The teacher *was helping* **him**.   _____ _____ **helped** by the teacher.

5. Present Perfect

   a. The teacher *has helped* **Yoko**.   _____ _____ **helped** by the teacher.

   b. The teacher *has helped* **Joe**.   _____ _____ **helped** by the teacher.

6. Future

   a. The teacher *will help* **me**.   _____ _____ **helped** by the teacher.

   b. The teacher *is going to help* **us**.   _____ _____ **helped** by the teacher.

B 🎧 *Listen to the sentences and write the words and endings you hear. Listen to the sentences again as you check your answers.*

An office building at night

1. The janitors *clean* the building at night.

   The building ___is___ clean ___ed___ by the janitors at night.

2. Window washers *wash* the windows.

   The windows _____ wash _____ by window washers.

3. A window washer *is washing* a window right now.

   A window _____ wash _____ by a window washer right now.

4. The security guard *has checked* the offices.

The offices _____ check _____ by the security guard.

5. The security guard *discovered* an open window.

An open window _____ discover _____ by the security guard.

6. The security guard *found* an unlocked door.

An unlocked door _____ found by the security guard.

7. The owner *will visit* the building tomorrow.

The building _____ visit _____ by the owner tomorrow.

8. The owner *is going to announce* new parking fees.

New parking fees _____ announce _____ by the owner.

C *Change the verbs from active to passive. Do not change the tenses.*

$$be \quad + \quad \textbf{past participle}$$

1. Leo *mailed* the package.

The package __was__ _____ mailed _____ by Leo.

2. That company *employs* many people.

Many people _____ _____ by that company.

3. That company *has hired* Ellen.

Ellen _____ _____ by that company.

ABOVE MATERIAL FROM: FUNDAMENTALS OF ENGLISH GRAMMAR, FOURTH EDITION

4. The secretary *is going to fax* the letter.

The letters _____ _____ by the secretary.

5. A college student *bought* my old car.

My old car _____ _____ by a college student.

6. Mrs. Adams *will do* the work.

The work _____ _____ by Mrs. Adams.

7. The doctor *was examining* the patient.

The patient _____ _____ by the doctor.

ABOVE MATERIAL FROM: FUNDAMENTALS OF ENGLISH GRAMMAR, FOURTH EDITION

GRAMMAR

Causatives

USING CAUSATIVE VERBS: *MAKE, HAVE, GET*

a. I *made* my brother *carry* my suitcase. **b.** I *had* my brother *carry* my suitcase. **c.** I *got* my brother *to carry* my suitcase.	***Make, have,*** and ***get*** can be used to express the idea that "X" causes "Y" to do something. When they are used as causative verbs, their meanings are similar but not identical. In (a): My brother had no choice. I insisted that he carry my suitcase. In (b): My brother carried my suitcase because I asked him to. In (c): I managed to persuade my brother to carry my suitcase.
Forms X *makes* Y *do* something. (*simple form*) X *has* Y *do* something. (*simple form*) X *gets* Y *to do* something. (*infinitive*)	
Causative *make*	
d. Mrs. Lee *made* her son *clean* his room. **e.** Sad movies *make* me *cry*.	Causative ***make*** is followed by the simple form of a verb, not an infinitive. *INCORRECT:* She made him ~~to~~ clean his room. ***Make*** gives the idea that "X" **gives "Y" no choice.** In (d): Mrs. Lee's son had no choice.

Causative *have*	
f. I *had* the plumber *repair* the leak. **g.** Jane *had* the waiter *bring* her some tea.	Causative ***have*** is followed by the simple form of a verb, not an infinitive. *INCORRECT:* I had him ~~to~~ repair the leak. ***Have*** gives the idea that "X" **requests** "Y" to do something. In (f): The plumber repaired the leak because I asked him to.
Causative *get*	
h. The students *got* the teacher *to dismiss* class early. **i.** Jack *got* his friends *to play* soccer with him after school.	Causative ***get*** is followed by an infinitive. ***Get*** gives the idea that "X" **persuades** "Y" to do something. In (h): The students managed to persuade the teacher to let them leave early.
Passive causatives	
j. I *had* my watch *repaired* (by someone). **k.** I *got* my watch *repaired* (by someone).	The past participle is used after ***have*** and ***get*** to give a passive meaning. In this case, there is usually little or no difference in meaning between ***have*** and ***get***. In (j) and (k): I caused my watch to be repaired by someone.

A *Choose the meaning that is closest to the meaning of the verb in* **boldface**.

1. The teacher **had** her class write a composition.
   a. gave them no choice   **b.** persuaded them   **c.** requested them to do this

2. Mrs. Wilson **made** the children wash their hands before dinner.
   a. gave them no choice   **b.** persuaded them   **c.** requested them to do this

3. Kostas **got** some neighborhood kids to help him clean out his garage.
   a. gave them no choice   **b.** persuaded them   **c.** requested them to do this

4. My boss **made** me redo my report because he wasn't satisfied with it.
   a. gave me no choice   **b.** persuaded me   **c.** requested me to do this

5. I **got** Rosa to lend me some lunch money.
   a. gave her no choice   **b.** persuaded her   **c.** requested her to do this

6. The police officer **had** the driver get out of his car.
   a. gave him no choice   **b.** persuaded him   **c.** requested him to do this

 ABOVE MATERIAL FROM: UNDERSTANDING AND USING ENGLISH GRAMMAR, FOURTH EDITION

B *Complete the sentences with the correct form of the verbs in parentheses.*

1. I made my son (*wash*) _____wash_____ the windows before he could go outside to play.

2. Mrs. Crane had her house (*paint*) _____painted_____.

3. I went to the bank to have a check (*cash*) _____.

4. Tom had a bad headache yesterday, so he got his twin brother, Tim, (*go*) _____ to class for him. The teacher didn't know the difference.

5. When Scott went shopping, he found a jacket that he really liked. After he had the sleeves (*shorten*) _____, it fit him perfectly.

6. When my laptop stopped working, I took it to the computer store to have it (*fix*) _____.

7. Peeling onions always makes me (*cry*) _____.

8. Tom Sawyer was supposed to paint the fence, but he didn't want to do it. He was a very clever boy. Somehow he got his friends (*do*) _____ it for him.

9. We had a professional photographer (*take*) _____ pictures of everyone at the wedding. We had over 500 pictures (*take*) _____.

ABOVE MATERIAL FROM: **UNDERSTANDING AND USING ENGLISH GRAMMAR, FOURTH EDITION**

C *Complete each sentence with a causative.*

1. (have / call) Why don't you _____ your assistant _____ them?

2. (get / do) I'll never be able to _____ my brother _____ the laundry.

3. (have / clean) Why didn't you _____ your friends _____ up after the party?

4. (get / give) You should _____ the hotel _____ you your money back.

5. (make / wash) Why don't you _____ your brother _____ the dishes?

6. (get / sign) I'm sure we can _____ the teacher _____ these forms.

VOCABULARY

A 🎧 Some Ways to Help Out Another Person

Read and Listen. Then listen again and repeat.

My car's at the repair shop. Could you possibly *give me a ride* to work?

I need to use the men's room. Could you *keep an eye on my things* till I get back?

Excuse me. Would you mind *lending me your pen?*

I can't play soccer this afternoon. You're a good player. Do you think you could *fill in for me?*

I'm too busy to go out for lunch. Do you think you could *pick up a sandwich* for me?

give [someone] **a ride**

keep an eye on [something or someone]

lend [someone] [something]

fill in for [someone]

pick up [something or someone]

B *Complete each sentence with one of the verb phrases from the Vocabulary.*

1. The meeting doesn't end until 5:00. Do you think you could _____ my kids from school at 4:00?

2. Janus usually answers the phones but he's out sick today. Could you possibly _____ him?

3. Oops. I'm completely out of cash! Do you think you could _____ me some money for lunch?

4. I have to make an important phone call. Could you _____ my daughter for about ten minutes?

5. Doris is catching a flight at 9:00. Do you think you might be able to _____ her _____ to the airport?

ABOVE MATERIAL FROM: TOP NOTCH 3, SECOND EDITION

CONVERSATION MODEL

A 🎧 *Read and listen to someone asking for a favor.*

A: Martin, I wonder if you could do me a favor.

B: Sure. What do you need?

A: My car's at the repair shop and I need to pick it up at 3:00. Do you think you could give me a ride?

B: I would, but I have a doctor's appointment at 2:00.

A: Oh, that's OK. <u>I understand.</u>

B: Maybe you could get Jack to take you.

A: Good idea.

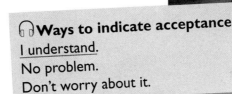

🎧 **Ways to indicate acceptance**
<u>I understand.</u>
No problem.
Don't worry about it.

B 🎧 **RHYTHM AND INTONATION**

Listen again and repeat. Then practice the Conversation Model with a partner.

C REVIEW THE VOCABULARY

On a separate sheet of paper, write a list of three requests for a favor.

D PAIR WORK

Change the Conversation Model to create a new conversation. Use one of the favors from your list. Your partner gives a reason for turning down your request and suggests getting someone else to do it. Then change roles.

I wonder if you could do me a favor …

A: _____, I wonder if you could do me a favor.

B: _____. What do you need?

A: _____. Do you think you could _____?

B: I would, but _____.

A: Oh, that's OK. _____.

B: Maybe you could get _____.

A: _____.

Reasons to turn down a request
- I'm running late for an appointment.
- I have a meeting in an hour.
- I'm expecting an important phone call.
- Your own reason: _____

Don't stop!
Make other suggestions.
What about __?
Why don't you ask __?

E CHANGE PARTNERS

Try to get someone else to do you a favor.

GOAL Request Express Service

VOCABULARY

A 🎧 SERVICES

Read and listen. Then listen again and repeat.

1. dry-clean a suit

2. repair shoes

3. frame a picture

4. deliver a package

5. shorten a / lengthen skirt

6. print a sign

7. copy a report

B PAIR WORK

Name other things you can get these services for.

> "You can also dry-clean sweaters or pants."

THE PASSIVE CAUSATIVE

Use the passive causative to talk about services you arrange for someone to do for you.

Use **have** or **get** + object + past participle.

> I **had the house repainted.**
>
> I**'m getting the grass cut** this afternoon.

GRAMMAR

The passive causative

Use a form of <u>have</u> or <u>get</u> with an object and a past participle to talk about arranging services. There is no difference in meaning between <u>have</u> and <u>get</u>.

	object	past participle
I **had**	my suits	**dry-cleaned**.
They're **having**	the office	**painted** tomorrow.
She **can get**	her sandals	**repaired** in an hour.

Remember: In the passive voice, a <u>by</u> phrase is used when the information is important.
We had the office painted last week. It looks great. (no <u>by</u> phrase)
We're having the office painted **by Royal Painting Services**. They're the best!

A *Write questions using the passive causative. Write three questions with **have** and three with **get**.*

1. Would it be possible to / these pictures / frame?

   _____

2. Could I / these sandals / repair / here?

   _____

3. Where can I / this bowl / gift wrap?

   _____

4. Can I / these shirts / dry-clean / by tomorrow?

   _____

5. Is it possible to / my hair / cut / at 3:00 / by George?

   _____

6. Would you / these photos / print / before 6:00?

   _____

B 🎧 *Listen to the conversations. Complete each statement with the item and the service. Use passive causatives.*

1. She needs to get her _____ _____.

2. He wants to get his _____ _____.

3. She's thinking about having a _____ _____.

4. He needs to have his _____ _____.

CONVERSATION MODEL

A 🎧 *Read and listen to someone requesting express service.*

A: Do you think I could get this jacket dry-cleaned by tomorrow?

B: Tomorrow? That might be difficult.

A: I'm sorry, but it's pretty urgent. My friend is getting married this weekend.

B: Well, I'll see what I can do. But it won't be ready until after 4:00.

A: I really appreciate it. Thanks!

B 🎧 RHYTHM AND INTONATION

Listen again and repeat. Then practice the Conversation Model with a partner.

C PAIR WORK

Change the Conversation Model. Use the ideas to request an express service and give a reason for why it's urgent. Then change roles.

A: Do you think I could _____ by _____?

B: _____? That might be difficult.

A: I'm sorry, but it's pretty urgent. _____.

B: Well, I'll see what I can do. But it won't be ready until _____.

A: _____!

Ideas for express services
- frame a [photo / painting / drawing / diploma]
- dry-clean a [suit / dress / sweater]
- lengthen or shorten a [dress / skirt / pants]

Ideas for why it's urgent
- Someone is coming to visit.
- You're going on [a vacation / a business trip].
- There's going to be [a party / a meeting].
- Your own idea: _____

Don't stop!
- Say you need to have the service completed earlier.
- Ask how much it will cost.

♻️ **Be sure to recycle this language.**

I owe you one!   I know this is last minute.
Thanks a million.   I won't keep you any longer.
You're a lifesaver!

D CHANGE PARTNERS

Request other express services.

ABOVE MATERIAL FROM: TOP NOTCH 3, SECOND EDITION

LISTENING AND DISCUSSION

A 🎧 *Listen to each conversation. Write a sentence to describe what the customer needs and when. Listen again if necessary.*

EXAMPLE: He'd like to get his shoes shined by tomorrow morning.

1. _____.
2. _____.
3. _____.
4. _____.

B *Work in small groups. Think about other cultures. Discuss the types of things people do or get done in order to change their appearance. Report back to your class.*

Some procedures to think about:

- **eyes:** lengthening eyelashes, coloring eyebrows

- **teeth:** straightening, whitening

- **face:** shortening nose, plumping lips

- **hair:** coloring, lengthening, styling, curling, straightening, braiding

- **skin:** whitening, tanning, tattooing, painting

- **hands / feet:** painting nails, painting hands or soles of feet

EXAMPLE: **A:** In India, women get their hands painted for special occasions. I think it looks nice.

B: In Japan, . . .

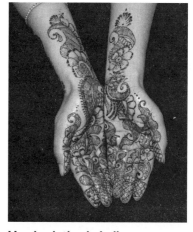

Hand painting in India

UNIT 2

Eating Well

GOALS By the end of Unit 2, you will be able to:

1 Talk about food likes and dislikes.

2 Talk about past habits.

A 1. *What kinds of food do you usually eat: healthful food or junk food?*

2. *Which foods did you love as a child?*

3. *Which foods did you dislike as a child?*

HEALTHY EATING PYRAMID

The right balance of foods will keep you healthy.

fats, oils, sweets
(rarely)

dairy
2–3 servings
per day for
calcium

meat, fish, beans
2–3 servings per day for
protein and vitamins

fruit
2–4 servings per
day for vitamins
and fiber

vegetables
3–5 servings per
day for vitamins
and fiber

**bread, grains,
pasta**
6–11 servings per
day for carbohydrates

Daily Exercise and Weight Control

Glossary

calcium: dairy products and
leafy green vegetables
provide calcium for healthy
bones and teeth.
carbohydrates: grains, pasta,
and bread are sources of
healthy carbohydrates.
protein: meat, fish, poultry,
eggs, legumes, and nuts are
rich sources of protein.
vitamins: vitamins A, B, C,
and D come from a variety
of foods and they are
important for good health.

B *Complete your own food pyramid to show how **you** eat. Compare pyramids with a partner.*

C *How is the Healthy Eating Pyramid different from your pyramid? Which do you think is a healthier diet? Explain.*

D 🎧 **PHOTO STORY**

Read and listen to people talking about food choices.

Rita: Didn't you tell me you were avoiding sweets?

Joy: I couldn't resist! I had a craving for chocolate.

Rita: Well, I have to admit it looks pretty good. How many calories are in that thing anyway?

Joy: I have no idea. Want to try some?

Rita: Thanks. But I think I'd better pass. I'm avoiding carbs.*

Joy: You? I don't believe it. You never used to turn down chocolate!

Rita: I know. But I'm watching my weight now.

*carbs (informal) = carbohydrates

Joy: Come on! It's really good.

Rita: OK. Maybe just a bite.

Joy: Hey, you only live once!

E *Find an underlined sentence or phrase in the Photo Story with the same meaning as each of the following.*

1. I don't know. _____

2. I should say no. _____

3. I couldn't stop myself. _____

4. I'm trying not to get heavier. _____

5. I really wanted. _____

6. I agree. _____

7. say no to. _____

8. I'll try a little. _____

F DISCUSSION

Read the descriptions of the diets. Would you ever try any of them? Why or why not?

The High-Fiber Diet
For maintaining better health, preventing disease, and watching weight. Eat anything you want. Be sure to consume 25 to 40 grams of fiber per day from grains, fruits, beans, and vegetables.

The Vegan Diet
For better health and prevention of disease. Avoid all animal products, including dairy and eggs. Eat lots of grains, beans, vegetables, and fruits.

The Atkins Diet
A high-protein, low-carbohydrate weight-loss diet. Eat foods such as meat, eggs, and cheese that are high in protein and fat. Avoid foods that are high in carbohydrates, such as starchy vegetables, bread, grains, sugar, and dairy products (except cheese, cream, and butter).

The Low-Fat Diet
For weight loss and the prevention of disease. Cut back fat to 20 to 30 percent of daily calories. Limit cholesterol in food to less than 300 mg per day (about the amount in one large egg).

I don't believe in the Atkins Diet. It has too much fat for me.

GOAL   Talk About Food Passions

VOCABULARY

A 🎧 FOOD PASSIONS

Read and listen. Then listen again and repeat.

I'm **crazy about** seafood.
I'm **a big** meat **eater.**
I'm **a big** coffee **drinker.**
I'm **a** chocolate **addict.**
I'm **a** pizza **lover.**

I **can't stand** fish.
I'm **not crazy about** chocolate.
I **don't care for** steak.
I'm **not much of a** pizza **eater.**
I'm **not much of a** coffee **drinker.**

B 🎧 *Circle the correct words to complete each statement about the speakers' food passions.*

1. She (is crazy about / doesn't care for) sushi.

2. He (loves / can't stand) asparagus.

3. She (is a mango lover / doesn't care for mangoes).

4. He (is a big pasta eater / isn't crazy about pasta).

5. She (is an ice cream addict / can't stand ice cream).

asparagus

sushi

ice cream

mangoes

pasta

ABOVE MATERIAL FROM: TOP NOTCH 2, SECOND EDITION

GRAMMAR

EXPRESSING PAST HABIT: *USED TO*

a. I *used to live* with my parents. Now I live in my own apartment. **b.** Ann *used to be* afraid of dogs, but now she likes dogs. **c.** Al *used to smoke*, but he doesn't anymore.	*Used to* expresses a past situation or habit that no longer exists at present. FORM: *used to* + *the simple form of a verb*
d. *Did* you *use to live* in Paris?	QUESTION FORM: *did* + *subject* + *use to*
e. I *didn't use to drink* coffee at breakfast, but now I always have coffee in the morning. **f.** I *never used to drink* coffee at breakfast, but now I always have coffee in the morning.	NEGATIVE FORM: *didn't use to* *Didn't use to* occurs infrequently. More commonly, people use *never* to express a negative idea with *used to*, as in (f).

ABOVE MATERIAL FROM: FUNDAMENTALS OF ENGLISH GRAMMAR, FOURTH EDITION

PRONUNCIATION

🎧 SOUND REDUCTION: USED TO

Notice how the pronunciation of to in used to changes to /tə/. Read and listen. Then listen again and repeat. Then practice the sentences on your own.

1. I used to be a big meat eater.
2. Jack used to like sweets.
3. Sally used to be crazy about fries.
4. They didn't use to like seafood.

CONVERSATION MODEL

A 🎧 *Read and listen to two people talk about their food passions.*

A: Are you a big coffee drinker?

B: Definitely. I'm crazy about coffee. What about you?

A: I used to have it a lot. But I've been cutting back.

B: Well, I couldn't live without it.

B 🎧 **RHYTHM AND INTONATION**

Listen again and repeat. Then practice the Conversation Model with a partner.

C *Complete the notepad with foods you like and dislike.*

Foods I'm crazy about	Foods I can't stand

D *Change the Conversation Model to role-play a conversation about food passions. Talk about foods and drinks you like and dislike. Talk about what you used to and didn't use to eat or drink. Start like this:*

A: Are you a big _____?

B: _____. What about you?

A: _____.

E *Change the Conversation Model again. Talk about other foods and drinks.*

GRAMMAR EXERCISES

A *Use the context to help you complete each sentence with* <u>used to</u> *or* <u>didn't use to</u>. *Then write two sentences about yourself.*

1. Gary _____ go out to eat a lot. But now he eats at home more often.

2. Nina _____ eat a lot of pasta. But now she does.

3. Vinnie _____ drink a lot of coffee. But now he's a coffee addict.

4. Anton _____ eat a lot of vegetables. But now he doesn't.

5. Cate _____ hate seafood. But now she's crazy about fish.

6. Ted _____ eat a lot of fatty foods. But now he avoids them.

7. Burt _____ drink a lot of water. But now he has several glasses a day.

8. May _____ like salads. But now she has salads several times a week.

9. (used to) I _____

   _____

10. (didn't use to) I _____

   _____

ABOVE MATERIAL FROM: TOP NOTCH 2, SECOND EDITION

B *Make sentences with a similar meaning by using* **used to**. *Some of the sentences are negative, and some of them are questions.*

1. *When I was a child, I was shy. Now I'm not shy.*

   I _____**used to be**_____ shy, but now I'm not.

2. *When I was young, I thought that people over 40 were old.*

   I _____ that people over 40 were old.

3. *Now you live in this city. Where did you live before you came here?*

   Where _____ ?

4. *Did you work for the phone company at some time in the past?*

   _____ for the phone company?

5. *When I was younger, I slept through the night. I never woke up in the middle of the night.*

   I _____ in the middle of the night, but now I do.

   I _____ through the night, but now I don't.

 ABOVE MATERIAL FROM: FUNDAMENTALS OF ENGLISH GRAMMAR, FOURTH EDITION

6. *When I was a child, I watched cartoons on TV. I don't watch cartoons anymore. Now I watch news programs.*

I _____ cartoons on TV, but I don't anymore.

I _____ news programs, but now I do.

7. *How about you?*

What _____ on TV when you were little?

C 🎧 ***Used to*** *is often pronounced "usta." Listen to the examples. Then complete the sentences with the non-reduced words you hear.*

> **EXAMPLES:** I used to (*usta*) ride my bike to work, but now I take the bus.
> I didn't use to (*usta*) be late when I rode my bike to work.
> Did you use to (*usta*) ride your bike to work?

1. I ___**used to stay**___ up past midnight, but now I often go to bed at 10:00 because I have an 8:00 class.

2. What time _____ to bed when you were a child?

3. Tom _____ tennis after work every day, but now he doesn't.

4. I _____ breakfast, but now I always have something to eat in the morning because I read that students who eat breakfast do better in school.

5. I _____ grammar, but now I do.

D *Edit the sentences. Correct the errors in verb tense usage.*

1. Alex used to ~~living~~ *live* in Cairo.

2. Junko used to worked for an investment company.

3. Margo was used to teach English, but now she works at a publishing company.

4. Where you used to live?

5. I didn't was used to get up early, but now I do.

6. Were you used to live in Singapore?

7. My family used to going to the beach every weekend, but now we don't.

E *Read about Kate's food passions. Then complete each sentence with* <u>used to</u> *or* <u>didn't use to</u> *and the verb.*

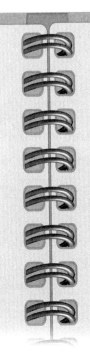

When I was a kid, I loved sweets. I think I ate about five cookies a day! When I was a teenager, I started eating a lot of meat. I had steaks and fries almost every day. I didn't care for vegetables or fruit. Then on my 20th birthday, I decided I needed a change, so I became a vegetarian. These days I eat meat again, but I avoid fatty foods and sugar. I've lost a lot of weight and I feel much better.

Kate

1. Kate _____ a lot of sweets, but now she avoids sugar.
   (eat)

2. When she was a teenager, she _____ fatty foods.
   (have)

3. Before she turned 20, she _____ vegetables.
   (like)

4. She _____ a vegetarian, but now she eats meat.
   (be)

5. Kate _____ care of herself, but now she eats well.
   (take)

F On a separate sheet of paper, write five sentences about things you used to or didn't use to do or think when you were younger. For example:

I didn't use to like coffee when I was younger.

GRAMMAR

A WARM-UP

Are the meanings of the two sentences the same or different?

1. When I was a child, I used to play in the street with the other children.

2. When I was a child, I would play in the street with the other children.

USING *WOULD* TO EXPRESS A REPEATED ACTION IN THE PAST

a. When I was a child, my father *would read* me a story at night before bedtime. **b.** When I was a child, my father *used to read* me a story at night before bedtime.	***Would*** can be used to express *an action that was repeated regularly in the past.* When **would** is used to express this idea, it has the same meaning as **used to** (*habitual past*). Sentences (a) and (b) have the same meaning.
c. I *used to live* in California. He *used to be* a Boy Scout. They *used to have* a Ford.	***Used to*** expresses *a situation that existed in the past,* as in (c). In this case, **would** may not be used as an alternative. **Would** is used only for regularly repeated *actions* in the past.

B Use **would** and the words in parentheses to express a repeated action in the past. Use **used to** to express a past situation.

1. I (*be*) _____ **used to be** _____ very shy. Whenever a stranger came to our house, I (*hide*)

   _____ **would hide** _____ in a closet.

2. I remember my Aunt Susan very well. Every time she came to our house, she (*give*) _____
   me a big kiss and pinch my cheek.

3. Illiteracy is still a problem in my country, but it (*be*) _____ much worse.

4. I (*be*) _____ afraid of flying. My heart (*start*) _____ pounding every time
   I stepped on a plane. But now I'm used to flying and enjoy it.

5. When I was a child, I (*take*) _____ a flashlight to bed with me so that I could read comic
   books without my parents knowing about it.

6. My sister (*live*) _____ in Montana, and when
   I visited her, we (*go*) _____ on weeklong
   backpacking trips in the mountains. Every morning, we (*wake*)
   _____ up to the sound of singing birds. During
   the day, we (*hike*) _____ through woods and along
   mountain streams. Often we (*see*) _____ deer.
   Once we saw a bear, but it went off in the opposite direction.

7. I (be) _____ an anthropology major. Once, I was a member of an archeological expedition. Every morning, we (get) _____ up before dawn. After breakfast, we (spend) _____ our entire day in the field. Sometimes one of us (find) _____ a particularly interesting item, perhaps an arrowhead or a piece of pottery. When that happened, other members of the group (gather) _____ around to see what had been unearthed.

ABOVE MATERIAL FROM: UNDERSTANDING AND USING ENGLISH GRAMMAR, FOURTH EDITION

C *Complete the sentences with* **would** *and a verb from the list. Use the words in parentheses.*

bring	fall	sleep	tell	wipe
come	listen	stay	throw	yell

1. I'll always remember Miss Emerson, my fifth-grade teacher. Sometimes a student _____ asleep in her class. Whenever that happened, Miss Emerson _____ a piece of chalk at the student!

2. My father never liked to talk on the phone. Whenever it rang, he (always) _____, "I'm not here!" Usually, he was only joking and _____ to the phone when it was for him.

3. I have fond childhood memories of my Aunt Betsy. Whenever she came to visit, she (always) _____ me a little present.

4. Some people have strange habits. For example, my Uncle Oscar, who lived with us when I was a child, (always) _____ his plate with his napkin whenever he sat down to a meal.

5. When I was in college, I acquired some bad habits. I didn't study until the night before a test, and then I _____ up all night studying. Then the next day after the test, I _____ all afternoon.

6. I'll never forget the wonderful evenings I spent with my grandparents when I was a child. My grandmother _____ stories of her childhood seventy years ago, and we _____ intently and question her for every detail.

ABOVE MATERIAL FROM: UNDERSTANDING AND USING ENGLISH GRAMMAR, 4TH ED WORKBOOK

D *If it is possible, complete the sentence with* <u>would</u>. *If not, use a form of* <u>used to</u>.

1. They _____ go to the beach every Saturday in the summer.

2. I _____ have a really large kitchen in my old house.

3. My husband never _____ like coffee, but now he can't get enough of it.

4. Almost every evening of our vacation we _____ eat at a terrific outdoor restaurant.

5. Before the microwave, people _____ heat up soup on the top of the stove.

ABOVE MATERIAL FROM: TOP NOTCH 2, SECOND EDITION

6. Sigrid _____ be a tour guide, but now she's a professional chef.

7. There _____ be three or four Italian restaurants in town, but now there aren't any.

ABOVE MATERIAL FROM: TOP NOTCH 2, SECOND EDITION

E *Work in small groups. Talk about how you used to be and how you are now. Answer the following questions. If you have a picture of yourself from that time, you can bring it in to class and show it to your group.*

- How did you use to look?

- What types of things would you do?

- How did you use to dress?

- Where did you use to live?

- What kinds of movies did you use to like?

- What did you use to do for fun?

- Where did you use to go on vacation?

- Who did you use to hang out with?

EXAMPLE: **A:** I used to have very long hair. Now I wear my hair short.

B: Anton, did you use to have long hair?

C: *Everybody* used to have long hair then.

ABOVE MATERIAL FROM: FOCUS ON GRAMMAR 3

GRAMMAR

USING BE *USED/ACCUSTOMED TO* AND *GET USED/ACCUSTOMED TO*

a. I *am used to* hot weather. **b.** I *am accustomed to* hot weather.	Examples (a) and (b) have the same meaning: "Living in a hot climate is usual and normal for me. I'm familiar with what it is like to live in a hot climate. Hot weather isn't strange or different to me."
c. I *am used **to living*** in a hot climate. **d.** I *am accustomed **to living*** in a hot climate.	Notice in (c) and (d): *to* (a preposition) is followed by the *-ing* form of a verb (a gerund).
e. I just moved from Florida to Alaska. I have never lived in a cold climate before, but I *am getting used to (accustomed to)* the cold weather here.	In (e): *I'm getting used to/accustomed to* = something is beginning to seem usual and normal to me.

A LOOKING AT GRAMMAR

Part I. Complete the sentences with *be used to*, affirmative or negative.

1. Juan is from Mexico. He _____ *is used to* _____ hot weather. He _____ *isn't used to* _____ cold weather.

2. Alice was born and raised in Chicago. She _____ living in a big city.

3. My hometown is New York City, but this year I'm going to school in a town with a population of 10,000.

I _____ living in a small town. I _____ living in a big city.

4. We do a lot of exercises in class. We _____ doing exercises.

Part II. Complete the sentences with *be accustomed to*, affirmative or negative.

5. Spiro recently moved to Hong Kong from Greece. He __*is accustomed to*__ eating Greek food.

He __*isn't accustomed to*__ eating Chinese food.

6. I always get up around 6:00 A.M. I _____ getting up early. I _____
sleeping late.

7. Our teacher always gives us a lot of homework. We _____ having a lot of homework every day.

8. Young schoolchildren rarely take multiple-choice tests. They _____
_____ taking that kind of test.

B 🎧 LISTENING AND SPEAKING

Part I. Complete the questions with the words you hear.

EXAMPLE: You will hear: What time are you accustomed to getting up?

You will write: __*are you accustomed to*__

1. What _____ doing in the evenings?

2. What time _____ going to bed?

3. What _____ having for breakfast?

4. _____ living in this area?

5. Do you live with someone or do you live alone? _____ that?

6. _____ speaking English every day?

7. What _____ doing on weekends?

8. What do you think about the weather here? _____ it?

Part II. Work with a partner. Take turns asking and answering the questions in Part I.

ABOVE MATERIAL FROM: FUNDAMENTALS OF ENGLISH GRAMMAR, FOURTH EDITION

C LET'S TALK: INTERVIEW

*Ask your classmates questions with **be used to/accustomed to**.*

EXAMPLE: buy \ frozen food
→ *Are you used to / accustomed to buying frozen food?*

1. get up \ early	**6.** drink \ coffee in the morning
2. sleep \ late	**7.** have \ dessert at night
3. eat \ breakfast	**8.** live \ in a big city
4. skip \ lunch	**9.** live \ in a small town
5. eat \ a late dinner	**10.** pay \ for all your expenses

D LET'S TALK

Work in small groups. Discuss one or more of the given topics. Make a list of your answers. Share some of them with the class.

Topics:

1. Junko is going to leave her parents' house next week. She is going to move in with two of her cousins who work in the city. Junko will be away from her home for the first time in her life. What is she going to have to get accustomed to?

2. Think of a time you traveled in or lived in a foreign country. What weren't you used to? What did you get used to? What didn't you ever get used to?

3. Think of the first day of a job you have had. What weren't you used to? What did you get used to?

GRAMMAR

A WARM-UP

Complete the sentences about food preferences. Make statements that are true for you.

1. There are some foods I liked when I was younger, but now I don't eat them. I used to eat

_____, but now I don't.

2. There are some foods I didn't like when I first tried them, but now they're okay. For example, the first time I

ate _____, I didn't like it, but now I'm used to eating them.

USED TO VS. BE USED TO

a. I *used to live* in Chicago, but now I live in Tokyo. INCORRECT: *I used to living in Chicago.* INCORRECT: *I am used to live in a big city.*	In (a): ***Used to*** expresses the habitual past. It is followed by the **simple form of a verb**.
b. I *am used to living* in a big city.	In (b): ***be used to*** is followed by the ***-ing* form of a verb** (a gerund).*

*NOTE: In both ***used to*** (habitual past) and ***be used to***, the "d" is not pronounced.

B LOOKING AT GRAMMAR

*Complete the sentences with an appropriate form of **be**. If no form of **be** is necessary, use **Ø**.*

1. I have lived in Malaysia for a long time. I _____ **am** _____ used to warm weather.

2. I _____ **Ø** _____ used to live in Portugal, but now I live in Spain.

3. I _____ used to sitting at this desk. I sit here every day.

4. I _____ used to sit in the back of the classroom, but now I prefer to sit in the front row.

5. When I was a child, I _____ used to play games with my friends in a big field near my house after school every day.

6. It's hard for my kids to stay inside on a cold, rainy day. They _____ used to playing outside in the big field near our house. They play there almost every day.

7. A teacher _____ used to answering questions. Students, especially good students, always have a lot of questions.

8. People _____ used to believe the world was flat.

C LOOKING AT GRAMMAR

*Complete the sentences with **used to/be used to** and the correct form of the verb in parentheses.*

1. Nick stays up later now than he did when he was in high school. He (go) _____ **used to go** _____ to bed at ten, but now he rarely gets to bed before midnight.

2. I got used to going to bed late when I was in college, but now I have a job and I need my sleep. These days I (go) _____ **am used to going** _____ to bed around ten-thirty.

3. I am a vegetarian. I (eat) _____ meat, but now I eat only meatless meals.

4. Ms. Wu has had a vegetable garden all her life. She (grow) _____ her own vegetables.

5. Oscar has lived in Brazil for ten years. He (eat) _____ Brazilian food. It's his favorite.

6. Georgio moved to Germany to open his own restaurant. He (have) _____ a small bakery in Italy.

7. I have taken the bus to work every day for the past five years. I (take) _____ _____ the bus.

8. Juanita travels by train on company business. She (go) _____ by plane, but now it's too expensive.

    ABOVE MATERIAL FROM: FUNDAMENTALS OF ENGLISH GRAMMAR, FOURTH EDITION

GRAMMAR

A WARM-UP

Choose the picture that matches the description.

One flower is gray. Another is orange. The other is white.

Picture A   Picture B

SINGULAR FORMS OF *OTHER*: *ANOTHER* VS. *THE OTHER*

Another	

a. There is a large bowl of apples on the table. Paul is going to eat one apple. If he is still hungry after that, he can eat *another apple*. There are many apples to choose from.	***Another*** means "one more out of a group of similar items, one in addition to the one(s) already mentioned." ***Another*** is a combination of *an* + *other*, written as one word.
The Other	

b. There are two apples on the table. Paul is going to eat one of them. Sara is going to eat *the other apple*.	***The other*** means "the last one in a specific group; the only one that remains from a given number of similar items."
c. Paul ate one apple. Then he ate { *another apple.* / *another one.* / *another.*	***Another*** and ***the other*** can be used as adjectives in front of a noun (e.g., *apple*) or in front of the word *one*. ***Another*** and ***the other*** can also be used alone as pronouns.
d. Paul ate one apple. Sara ate { *the other apple.* / *the other one.* / *the other.*	

ABOVE MATERIAL FROM: FUNDAMENTALS OF ENGLISH GRAMMAR, FOURTH EDITION

B LOOKING AT GRAMMAR

*Complete the sentences with **another** or **the other**.*

1. There are two birds in Picture A. One is an eagle. _____The other_____ is a chicken.

Picture A   Picture B

2. There are three birds in Picture B. One is an eagle.

   a. _____ one is a chicken.

   b. _____ bird is a crow.

3. There are many kinds of birds in the world. One kind is an eagle.

   a. _____ kind is a chicken.

   b. _____ kind is a crow.

   c. _____ kind is a sea gull.

   d. What is the name of _____ kind of bird in the world?

4. It rained yesterday, and from the look of those dark clouds, we're going to have _____ rainstorm today.

5. Nicole and Michelle are identical twins. The best way to tell them apart is by looking at their ears. One of them has pierced ears, and _____ doesn't.

6. France borders several countries. One is Spain. _____ is Italy.

GRAMMAR

A WARM-UP

Match the sentences to the correct pictures.

Picture A   Picture B

1. _____ Some are orange. Others are gray.

2. _____ Some are orange. The others are gray.

ABOVE MATERIAL FROM: FUNDAMENTALS OF ENGLISH GRAMMAR, FOURTH EDITION

Other(s)

There are many apples in Paul's kitchen. Paul is holding one apple.

a. There are **other** *apples* in a bowl.
 (adjective) + (noun)

b. There are **other** *ones* on a plate.
 (adjective) + ones

c. There are **others** on a chair.
 (pronoun)

Other(s) (without *the*) means "several more out of a group of similar items, several in addition to the one(s) already mentioned."

The adjective **other** (without an **-s**) can be used with a plural noun (e.g., *apples*) or with the word **ones**.

Others (with an **-s**) is a plural pronoun; it is not used with a noun.

In (c): **others** = **other apples**

The Other(s)

There are four apples on the table. Paul is going to take one of them.

d. Sara is going to take **the other** *apples*.
 (adjective) + (noun)

e. Sara is going to take **the other** *ones*.
 (adjective) + ones

f. Sara is going to take **the others**.
 (pronoun)

The other(s) means "the last ones in a specific group, the remains from a given number of similar items."

The other (without an **-s**) can be used as an adjective in front of a noun or the word **ones**, as in (d) and (e).

The others (with an **-s**) is a plural pronoun; it is not used with a noun.

In (f): **the others** = **the other apples**

B LOOKING AT GRAMMAR

Perform these actions.

1. Hold two pens. Use a form of ***other*** to describe the second pen.
   → *I'm holding two pens. One is mine, and the other belongs to Ahmed.*

2. Hold three pens. Use a form of ***other*** to describe the second and third pens.

3. Hold up your two hands. One of them is your right hand. Tell us about your left hand, using a form of ***other***.

4. Hold up your right hand. One of the five fingers is your thumb. Using forms of ***other***, tell us about your index finger, then your middle finger, then your ring finger, and then your little finger, the last of the five fingers on your right hand.

C LOOKING AT GRAMMAR

*Complete the sentences with **other(s)** or the **other(s)**.*

1. There are many kinds of animals in the world. The elephant is one kind. Some _____*others*_____ are tigers, horses, and bears.

2. There are many kinds of animals in the world. The elephant is one kind. Some _____ kinds are tigers, horses, and bears.

3. There are three colors in the Italian flag. One of the colors is red. _____ are green and white.

4. There are three colors in the Italian flag. One of the colors is red. _____ colors are green and white.

5. Many people like to get up very early in the morning. _____ like to sleep until noon.

6. There are many kinds of geometric figures. Some are circles. _____ figures are squares.

   Still _____ are rectangular.

7. There are four geometric figures in the above drawing. One is a square. _____ figures are a rectangle, a circle, and a triangle.

8. Of the four geometric figures in the drawing, only the circle has curved lines. _____ have straight lines.

   ABOVE MATERIAL FROM: FUNDAMENTALS OF ENGLISH GRAMMAR, FOURTH EDITION

D LET'S READ AND WRITE

Read the passage and answer the questions.

Calming Yourself

When was the last time you felt nervous or anxious? Were you able to calm yourself? There are a variety of techniques that people use to calm themselves. Here are three that many people have found helpful.

One way that people relax is by imagining a peaceful place, such as a tropical beach. Thinking about the warm water, cool breezes, and steady sounds of the ocean waves helps people calm themselves. Another popular method is deep breathing. Inhaling deeply and then slowly exhaling is an easy way for people to slow their heart rate and relax their body. Still other people find exercise helpful. Some people benefit from a slow activity like a 20-minute walk. Others prefer activities that make them tired, like running or swimming.

How about you? How do you calm yourself when you feel nervous? Do any of these methods help you, or do you do other things to relax?

1. What are three ways people relax when they are nervous? (Use *one* and *another* in your answer.)

2. Why do some people choose activities like running and swimming as a way to relax?

3. Imagine you are trying to relax by thinking of a peaceful place. What place would you think of?

4. How do you relax when you are nervous?

UNIT 3

Living with Computers

GOALS By the end of Unit 3, you will be able to:

1 Troubleshoot a problem.

2 Describe how you use computers.

3 Recommend a better deal.

4 Discuss the impact of the Internet.

A *Are you a person who gets excited about new technology, or does it make you nervous? Why?*

B *Do you know how to solve computer problems? Answer the questions by checking* <u>Yes</u>, <u>No</u>, *or* <u>Not sure</u>. *Then compare your answers with your partner and discuss some possible solutions.*

DO YOU KNOW WHAT TO DO IF . . .

	Yes	No	Not sure
1. you get a virus?	☐	☐	☐
2. your printer won't print?	☐	☐	☐
3. you can't log on to a website?	☐	☐	☐
4. your computer is really slow?	☐	☐	☐

Computer solutions
- run anti-virus software
- try rebooting
- contact a technical support expert
- check if it's turned on
- buy a new computer
- (your own idea) _____

C 🎧 PHOTO STORY

Read and listen to a conversation about a computer problem.

Amy: What are you doing here at this hour?
Dee: Fooling around on my new laptop.
Amy: Am I interrupting you?
Dee: Not at all. Paul and I are just instant messaging. What's up?
Amy: Well, I was wondering if you could help me with something.
Dee: Of course.

Amy: When I try to log on to my e-mail, nothing happens.
Dee: Are you sure you used the right password?
Amy: Absolutely. And I've never had a problem before.
Dee: Maybe you should try rebooting. Sometimes that takes care of it.
Amy: You mean just shutting down and restarting?
Dee: Right.

Amy: You think that would do it?
Dee: It couldn't hurt. Listen, Paul's still there. Let me send a quick response, OK? I'll just be a second.
Amy: I'm sorry. I'll go and try rebooting to see if that does the trick.

D *Look at the six underlined expressions in the Photo Story. Write each expression next to its meaning. (Two expressions have the same meaning.)*

1. won't take a long time _____

2. not doing anything serious _____

3. It doesn't work _____

4. It's worth trying _____

5. fixes the problem _____

6. fixes the problem _____

GOAL Troubleshoot a Problem

CONVERSATION MODEL

A 🎧 *Read and listen to people troubleshoot a computer problem.*

A: Eugene, could you take a look at this?

B: Sure. What's the problem?

A: Well, I clicked on the toolbar to save a file and the computer crashed.

B: Why don't you try restarting? That sometimes works.

A: OK. I'll give that a try.

B 🎧 RHYTHM AND INTONATION

Listen again and repeat. Then practice the Conversation Model with a partner.

🎧 **Ways to reassure someone**
That sometimes works.
That might help.
That may do the trick.

VOCABULARY

A COMPUTER TERMS AND COMMANDS

🎧 *Read and listen. Then listen again and repeat.*

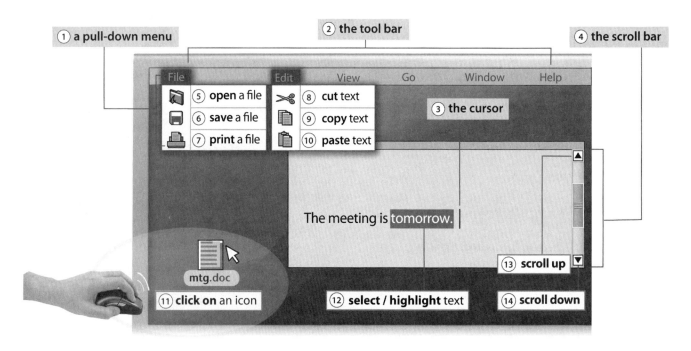

B 🎧 *Listen. Check the computer command each person needs.*

1. He needs to click on . . .
2. She needs to click on . . .
3. He needs to click on . . .
4. She needs to click on . . .
5. He needs to click on . . .
6. She needs to click on . . .

GRAMMAR

MAKING COMPARISONS WITH AS ... AS

a. Tina is 21 years old. Sam is also 21. Tina is *as old as* Sam (is). **b.** Mike came **as quickly as** he could.	**As . . . as** is used to say that the two parts of a comparison are equal or the same in some way. In (a): **as** + *adjective* + **as** In (b): **as** + *adverb* + **as**
c. Ted is 20. Tina is 21. Ted is *not as old as* Tina. **d.** Ted is *not quite as old as* Tina. **e.** Amy is 5. She is *not nearly as old as* Tina.	Negative form: **not as . . . as.*** **Quite** and **nearly** are often used with the negative. In (d): **not quite as . . . as** = a small difference. In (e): **not nearly as . . . as** = a big difference.
f. Sam is *just as old as* Tina. **g.** Ted is *nearly/almost as old as* Tina.	Common modifiers of **as . . . as** are **just** (meaning "exactly") and **nearly/almost.**

Tina 21   Sam 21   Ted 20   Amy 5

*Also possible: **not so . . . as:** *Ted is **not so old as** Tina.*

A *Complete the sentences, with **just as, almost as/not quite as**, or **not nearly as**.*

Part I. Compare the fullness of the glasses.

1. Glass 4 is <u>almost as / not quite as</u> full as Glass 2.

2. Glass 3 is _____ full as Glass 2.

3. Glass 1 is _____ full as Glass 2.

Part II. Compare the size of the boxes.

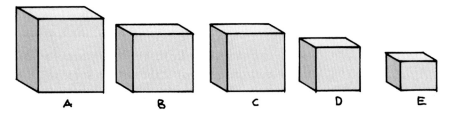

4. Box B is _____ big as Box A.

5. Box E is _____ big as Box A.

6. Box C is _____ big as Box B.

7. Box E is _____ big as Box D.

B *Complete the sentences with* **as . . . as** *and words from the list. Give your own opinion. Use negative verbs where appropriate.*

a housefly / an ant	good health / money
a lake / an ocean	honey / sugar
a lemon / a watermelon	monkeys /people
a lion / a tiger	reading a book / listening to music
a shower / a bath	the sun / the moon

1. _An ant isn't as_____ big as _a housefly_____.

2. _A lion is as_____ dangerous and wild as _a tiger_____.

3. _____ large as _____.

4. _____ sweet as _____.

5. _____ important as _____.

6. _____ quiet as _____.

7. _____ hot as _____.

8. _____ good at climbing trees as _____.

9. _____ relaxing as _____.

ABOVE MATERIAL FROM: FUNDAMENTALS OF ENGLISH GRAMMAR, FOURTH EDITION

C 🎧 *Complete the sentences with the words you hear.*

Sylvia 30   Brigita 28   Lara 50   Tanya 50

EXAMPLES: You will hear: Brigita isn't as old as Lara.

You will write: ___*isn't as old as*___

1. Lara _____ Tanya.

2. Sylvia _____ Lara.

3. Sylvia and Brigita _____ Tanya.

4. Brigita _____ Sylvia.

5. Brigita _____ Sylvia.

D 🎧 **PRONUNCIATION** *Stress in as ... as phrases*

Read and listen. Then listen again and repeat.

1. The new printer is as slow as the old one.

2. My old smart phone is just as small as the new one.

3. The X12 mouse isn't nearly as nice as the X30.

4. My keyboard didn't cost quite as much as the Z6.

E *Read the statements you wrote in Exercise B above aloud, paying attention to stress.*

CONVERSATION MODEL

A 🎧 *Listen to someone recommend a better deal.*

A: I'm thinking about getting a new monitor.

B: Oh, yeah? What kind?

A: Everyone says I should get a Macro.

B: Well, I've heard that the Panatel is as good as the Macro, but it costs a lot less.

A: Really? I'll check it out.

B 🎧 **RHYTHM AND INTONATION**

Listen again and repeat.

BEFORE YOU LISTEN

🎧 **VOCABULARY** Internet activities

Read and listen. Then listen again and repeat.

attach (a file) place a document or photo into an e-mail

upload (a file) move a document, music file, or picture from a personal computer, phone, or MP3 player onto the Internet

download (a file) move a document, music file, or picture from the Internet onto a personal computer, phone, or MP3 player

surf the Internet visit a lot of different websites on the Internet for information that interests you

join (an online group) become a member of an Internet group to meet friends and share information about your hobbies and interests

post (a message) add your comments to an online discussion on a message board, a blog, or a social networking site

ABOVE MATERIAL FROM: TOP NOTCH 2, SECOND EDITION

LISTENING COMPREHENSION

A 🎧 LISTEN FOR THE MAIN IDEA

Listen to people describing how they use the Internet. Write a check in the box next to the person who seems to enjoy the Internet the least. Explain your answer.

☐ **1** George Thomas   ☐ **2** Sonia Castro   ☐ **3** Robert Kuan   ☐ **4** Nadia Montasser

B 🎧 LISTEN FOR DETAILS

Listen again and check the activities each person does.

	George Thomas	**Sonia Castro**	**Robert Kuan**	**Nadia Montasser**
buys products	☐	☐	☐	☐
downloads music	☐	☐	☐	☐
keeps up with the news	☐	☐	☐	☐
participates in online groups	☐	☐	☐	☐
plays online games	☐	☐	☐	☐
sends instant messages	☐	☐	☐	☐
surfs the Internet	☐	☐	☐	☐
uploads photos	☐	☐	☐	☐
uses a computer at work	☐	☐	☐	☐

GRAMMAR

A WARM-UP

Do you agree or disagree with these statements? Circle yes or no.

1. I enjoy very cold weather.   yes   no

2. It's cooler today than yesterday.   yes   no

3. It's much warmer today than yesterday.   yes   no

4. It's a little hotter today than yesterday.   yes   no

MODIFYING COMPARATIVES

a. Tom is *very old*. **b.** Ann drives *very carefully*.	***Very*** often modifies adjectives, as in (a), and adverbs, as in (b).
c. INCORRECT: *Tom is very older than I am.* INCORRECT: *Ann drives very more carefully than she used to.*	***Very*** is NOT used to modify comparative adjectives and adverbs.
d. Tom is *much / a lot / far older* than I am. **e.** Ann drives *much / a lot / far more carefully* than she used to.	Instead, ***much***, ***a lot***, or ***far*** are used to modify comparative adjectives and adverbs, as in (d) and (e).
f. Ben is *a little* (*bit*) *older* than I am OR (*informally*) me.	Another common modifier is a ***little/a little bit***, as in (f).

B LOOKING AT GRAMMAR

*Add **very**, **much**, **a lot**, or **far** to the sentences.*

1. It's hot today. → *It's **very** hot today.*

2. It's hotter today than yesterday. → *It's **much/a lot/far** hotter today than yesterday.*

3. An airplane is fast.

4. Taking an airplane is faster than driving.

5. Learning a second language is difficult for many people.

6. Learning a second language is more difficult than learning chemistry formulas.

7. You can live more inexpensively in student housing than in a rented apartment.

8. You can live inexpensively in student housing.

GRAMMAR

A WARM-UP

Complete the sentences with your own words.

1. Compare the cost of two cars:

   (*A/An*) _____ is more expensive than (*a/an*) _____.

2. Compare the cost of two kinds of fruit:

   _____ are less expensive than _____.

3. Compare the cost of two kinds of shoes (boots, sandals, tennis shoes, flip-flops, etc.):

   _____ are not as expensive as _____.

COMPARISONS WITH *LESS . . . THAN* AND *NOT AS . . . AS*

MORE THAN ONE SYLLABLE:
  a. A pen is *less expensive than* a book.
  b. A pen is *not as expensive as* a book.
	The opposite of *-er/more* is expressed by *less* or *not as . . . as*.
	Examples (a) and (b) have the same meaning.

	Less and *not as . . . as* are used with adjectives and adverbs of **more than one syllable**.

ONE SYLLABLE:
  c. A pen is *not as large as* a book.
    INCORRECT: A pen is less large than a book.
	Only *not as . . . as* (NOT *less*) is used with **one-syllable adjectives or adverbs**, as in (c).

B LOOKING AT GRAMMAR

Circle the correct completion(s) for each sentence.

1. My nephew is _____ old _____ my niece.
     a. less . . . than   **b.** not as . . . as

2. My nephew is _____ hard-working _____ my niece.
     a. less . . . than   **b.** not as . . . as

3. A bee is _____ big _____ a bird.
     a. less . . . than   **b.** not as . . . as

4. My brother is _____ interested in computers _____ I am.
     a. less . . . than   **b.** not as . . . as

5. Some students are _____ serious about their schoolwork _____ others.
     a. less . . . than   **b.** not as . . . as

6. I am _____ good at repairing things _____ Diane is.
     a. less . . . than   **b.** not as . . . as

C GAME

*Work in teams. Compare the given words using **(not) as . . . as**, **less**, and **more/-er**. How many comparison sentences can you think of? The team with the most correct sentences wins.*

EXAMPLE: trees and flowers (*big, colorful, useful, etc.*)
→ *Trees are bigger than flowers.*
→ *Flowers are usually more colorful than trees.*
→ *Flowers are less useful than trees.*
→ *Flowers aren't as tall as trees.*

1. the sun and the moon
2. teenagers and adults
3. two restaurants in this area
4. two famous people in the world

ABOVE MATERIAL FROM: FUNDAMENTALS OF ENGLISH GRAMMAR, FOURTH EDITION

D 🎧 *Listen to the conversations. Check the box if the person recommends the product. Then listen again and infer how to complete each statement.*

Recommended?
☐ the C40 computer
☐ the Hip web camera
☐ the new Mundite CD drive
☐ the Play Zone 3 game

1. The C40's monitor is _____ the X8's.
   a. the same size as   **b.** larger than   **c.** smaller than

2. The Hip web camera is _____ the Pentac web camera.
   a. the same price as   **b.** cheaper than   **c.** more expensive than

3. Mundite's new CD drive is _____ Mundite's old CD drive.
   a. the same as   **b.** faster than   **c.** slower than

4. Play Zone 3 is _____ Play Zones 1 and 2.
   a. the same as   **b.** less fun than   **c.** more fun than

ABOVE MATERIAL FROM: TOP NOTCH 2, SECOND EDITION

E Game

As . . . as is used in many traditional phrases. These phrases are generally spoken rather than written. See how many of them you're familiar with by completing the sentences with the given words. Work in teams. The team with the most correct answers wins.

✓ a bear	a cat	a hornet	a mule	an ox
a bird	a feather	a kite	a rock	the hills

1. When will dinner be ready? I'm **as** hungry **as** _____ *a bear* _____.

2. Did Toshi really lift that heavy box all by himself? He must be **as** strong **as** _____.

3. It was a lovely summer day. School was out, and there was nothing in particular that I had to do. I felt **as** free **as** _____.

4. Marco won't change his mind. He's **as** stubborn **as** _____.

5. How can anyone expect me to sleep in this bed? It's **as** hard **as** _____.

6. Of course I've heard that joke before! It's **as** old **as** _____.

7. Why are you walking back and forth? What's the matter? You're **as** nervous **as** _____.

8. Thanks for offering to help, but I can carry the box alone. It looks heavy, but it isn't. It's **as** light **as** _____.

9. When Erica received the good news, she felt **as** high **as** _____.

10. **A:** Was he angry?

    B: You'd better believe it! He was **as** mad **as** _____.

ox

mule

hornet

UNIT 4

Health Matters

GOALS By the end of Unit 4, you will be able to:

1 Call in sick.

2 Make a medical or dental appointment.

3 Talk about medications.

A *Do you think the information on the website is useful? Why do you think some people wait until they get back home to see a dentist?*

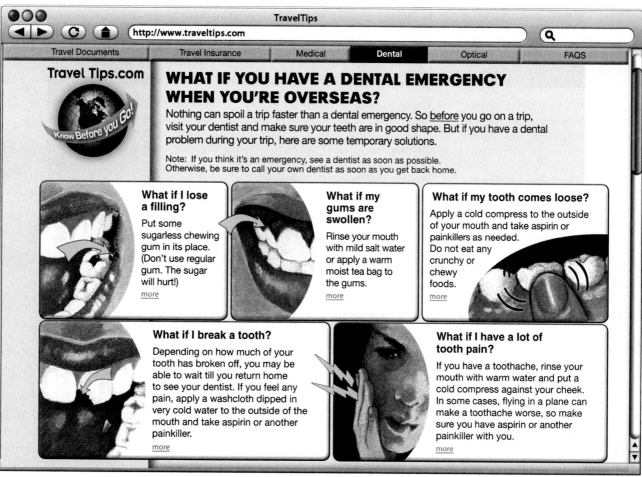

Information source: www.webmd.com

B PAIR WORK

Discuss each of the situations described in the website and what you would do. Circle yes or no.

I would . . .

• ignore the problem.		yes	no
• make an appointment to see a dentist right away.		yes	no
• call or e-mail my own dentist and ask for advice.		yes	no
• use the remedy suggested in the website.		yes	no
• use my own remedy (explain).		yes	no

C 🎧 PHOTO STORY

Read and listen to someone with a dental emergency during a trip.

Guest: I need to see a dentist as soon as possible. I think it's an emergency. I was wondering if you might be able to recommend someone who speaks English.
Clerk: Let me check. Actually, there is one not far from here. Would you like me to make an appointment for you?
Guest: If you could. Thanks. I'm in a lot of pain.

Dentist: So I hear you're from overseas.
Patient: From Ecuador. Thanks for fitting me in.
Dentist: Luckily, I had a cancellation. So what brings you in today?
Patient: Well, this tooth is killing me.

Dentist: When did it first begin to hurt?
Patient: It's been bothering me since last night.
Dentist: Let's have a look. Open wide.
Patient: Ah . . .
Dentist: Well, let's take an X-ray and see what's going on.

D *Find the underlined statements in the Photo Story. Then use the context to help you restate each one in your own words.*

1. I was wondering if you might be able to recommend someone who speaks English.

2. If you could. Thanks.

3. Thanks for fitting me in.

4. This tooth is killing me.

5. It's been bothering me since last night.

6. Let's have a look.

7. Let's take an X-ray and see what's going on.

E *Have you—or has someone you know—ever had an emergency that required dental or medical attention? Complete the chart.*

Where did it happen?	When did it happen?	What happened?

F GROUP WORK

Tell your classmates about your emergency.

> "Last year, I went skiing and I broke my arm. I had to go to the emergency room at the hospital."

GOAL   Call in Sick

VOCABULARY

A 🎧 SYMPTOMS

Read and listen. Then listen again and repeat.

I feel . . .

| dizzy | nauseous | weak | short of breath |

I've been . . .

vomiting

coughing

sneezing

wheezing

I have pain . . .

in my chest

in my hip

in my ribs

in my stomach

B PAIR WORK

Discuss what you would suggest to someone with some of the symptoms in the Vocabulary.

> "If you feel dizzy, you should lie down."

C 🎧 *Listen and check the symptoms each patient describes. Then listen again. If the patient has pain, write where it is.*

	dizziness	nausea	weakness	vomiting	coughing	sneezing	wheezing	pain	If pain, where?
1.	☐	☐	☐	☐	☐	☐	☐	☐	
2.	☐	☐	☐	☐	☐	☐	☐	☐	
3.	☐	☐	☐	☐	☐	☐	☐	☐	
4.	☐	☐	☐	☐	☐	☐	☐	☐	
5.	☐	☐	☐	☐	☐	☐	☐	☐	
6.	☐	☐	☐	☐	☐	☐	☐	☐	

PRONUNCIATION

A 🎧 INTONATION OF LISTS

Use rising intonation on each item before the last item in a list. Use falling intonation on the last item. Read and listen. Then listen again and repeat.

1. I feel weak and dizzy.

2. I've been sneezing, coughing, and wheezing.

3. I have pain in my neck, my shoulders, my back, and my hip.

GRAMMAR

THE FORM OF MODAL AUXILIARIES

The verbs listed below are called "modal auxiliaries." They are helping verbs that express a wide range of meanings (ability, permission, possibility, necessity, etc.). Most of the modals have more than one meaning.

Auxiliary + the Simple Form of a Verb

can	**a.**	Olga *can speak* English.	*Can, could, may, might, should, had better, must, will,* and *would* are immediately followed by the simple form of a verb.
could	**b.**	He *couldn't come* to class.	
may	**c.**	It *may rain* tomorrow.	
might	**d.**	It *might rain* tomorrow.	• They are not followed by **to**.
should	**e.**	Mary *should study* harder.	INCORRECT: *Olga can to speak English.*
had better	**f.**	I *had better study* tonight.	• The main verb does not have a final *-s*.
must	**g.**	Billy! You *must listen* to me!	INCORRECT: *Olga can speaks English.*
will	**h.**	I *will be* in class tomorrow.	• The main verb is not in a past form.
would	**i.**	*Would* you please *close* the door?	INCORRECT: *Olga can spoke English.*
			• The main verb is not in its *-ing* form.
			INCORRECT: *Olga can speaking English.*

Auxiliary + to + the Simple Form of a Verb

have to	**j.**	I *have to study* tonight.	***To*** *+ the simple form* is used with these auxiliaries: *have to, have got to, be able to,* and *ought to.*
have got to	**k.**	I *have got to study* tonight.	
be able to	**l.**	Kate *is able to study* harder.	
ought to	**m.**	Kate *ought to study* harder.	

A LOOKING AT GRAMMAR

Make sentences with the given verbs + **come.** *Add* **to** *where necessary. Use this model:* Leo _____ tonight.

EXAMPLE: can → *Leo can come tonight.*

1. may
2. should
3. ought
4. will not
5. could not
6. might
7. had better
8. has
9. has got
10. is not able

GRAMMAR

EXPRESSING POSSIBILITY: *MAY, MIGHT,* AND *MAYBE;*
EXPRESSING PERMISSION: *MAY AND CAN*

a. It *may rain* tomorrow. **b.** It *might rain* tomorrow. **c.** — Why isn't John in class? — I don't know. He $\left\{ \begin{array}{l} \textit{may} \\ \textit{might} \end{array} \right\}$ be sick today.	*May* and *might* express *possibility* in the present or future. They have the same meaning. There is no difference in meaning between (a) and (b).
d. It *may not rain* tomorrow. **e.** It *might not rain* tomorrow.	Negative: *may not* and *might not* (Do not contract *may* and *might* with *not*.)
f. *Maybe* it will rain tomorrow. COMPARE: **g.** *Maybe* John is sick. (*adverb*) **h.** John *may be* sick. (*verb*)	In (f) and (g): *maybe* (spelled as one word) is an adverb. It means "possibly." It comes at the beginning of a sentence. *INCORRECT: It will maybe rain tomorrow.* In (h): *may be* (two words) is a verb form: the auxiliary *may* + *the main verb* ***be***. Examples (g) and (h) have the same meaning. *INCORRECT: John maybe sick.*
i. Yes, children, you *may have* a cookie after dinner. **j.** Okay, kids, you *can have* a cookie after dinner.	*May* is also used to give *permission*, as in (i). *Can* is often used to give *permission*, too, as in (j). NOTE: Examples (i) and (j) have the same meaning, but *may* is more formal than *can*.
k. You *may not have* a cookie. You *can't have* a cookie.	*May not* and *cannot* (*can't*) are used to deny permission (i.e., to say "no").

A *Complete the sentences with* **can, may,** *or* **might.** *Identify the meaning expressed by the modals: possibility or permission.*

In a courtroom for a speeding ticket

1. No one speaks without the judge's permission. You _____ may / can _____ not speak until the judge asks you a question.

   Meaning: _____ permission _____

2. The judge _____ reduce your fine for your speeding ticket, or she _____ not. It depends.

   Meaning: _____

3. You _____ not argue with the judge. If you argue, you will get a fine.

   Meaning: _____

4. You have a strong case, but I'm not sure if you will convince the judge. You _____ win or you _____ lose.

   Meaning: _____

ABOVE MATERIAL FROM: FUNDAMENTALS OF ENGLISH GRAMMAR, FOURTH EDITION

BEFORE YOU LISTEN

A 🎧 VOCABULARY *Medications*

Read and listen. Then listen again and repeat.

a prescription

PATIENT NAME

🎧 Medicine label information
Dosage: Take 1 tablet by mouth every day.
Warnings: Do not take while driving or operating machinery.
Side effects: May cause dizziness or nausea.

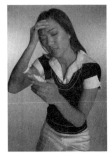

a painkiller

cold tablets

a nasal spray /
a decongestant

eye drops

an antihistamine

cough medicine

an antibiotic

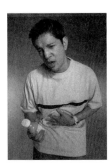

an antacid

an ointment

vitamins

B PAIR WORK

Discuss what you might use each medication for.

"I might take an antacid
for a stomachache."

LISTENING COMPREHENSION

🎧 *Listen to each conversation with a doctor. Use the medications vocabulary on page 57 and the symptoms vocabulary from pages 53–54 to complete the chart for each patient.*

Name: __Didem Yilmaz__

What are the patient's symptoms?

Is the patient currently taking any medications? ☐ Yes ☐ No

If so, which ones?

Did the patient get a prescription? ☐ Yes ☐ No

Name: __Lucy Fernández__

What are the patient's symptoms?

Is the patient currently taking any medications? ☐ Yes ☐ No

If so, which ones?

Did the patient get a prescription? ☐ Yes ☐ No

Name: __Mark Goh__

What are the patient's symptoms?

Is the patient currently taking any medications? ☐ Yes ☐ No

If so, which ones?

Did the patient get a prescription? ☐ Yes ☐ No

CONVERSATION MODEL

A 🎧 *Read and listen to someone making an appointment.*

A: Hello. Doctor Star's office. Can I help you?

B: Hello. I need to make an appointment for a blood test. I wonder if I might be able to come in early next week.

A: Let's see if I can fit you in. How about Tuesday?

B: Could I come in the morning?

A: Let me check . . . Would you be able to be here at 10:00?

B: That would be perfect.

A: We'll see you then.

B: Thanks! I really appreciate it.

B 🎧 **RHYTHM AND INTONATION**

Listen again and repeat. Then practice the Conversation Model with a partner.

ABOVE MATERIAL FROM: TOP NOTCH 3, SECOND EDITION

C PAIR WORK

Make an appointment to see a doctor or dentist. Suggest a day.
Write the appointment on the schedule. Then change roles.

A: Hello. Doctor _____'s office. Can I help you?

B: Hello. I need to make an appointment for _____.
I wonder if I might be able to come in _____.

A: Let's see if I can fit you in. Would you be able to be here at _____?

B: _____.

Don't stop!
- Say you can't be there today.
- Discuss other days and times.

Ideas
- tomorrow
- next week
- early next week
- at the end of next week
- the week of [the 3rd]

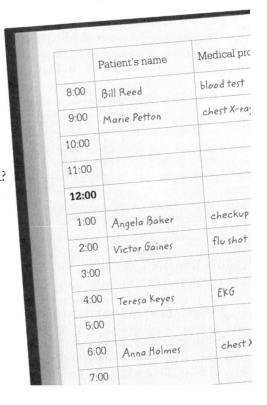

	Patient's name	Medical pro
8:00	Bill Reed	blood test
9:00	Marie Petton	chest X-ray
10:00		
11:00		
12:00		
1:00	Angela Baker	checkup
2:00	Victor Gaines	flu shot
3:00		
4:00	Teresa Keyes	EKG
5:00		
6:00	Anna Holmes	chest X
7:00		

D CHANGE PARTNERS

Make another appointment.

ABOVE MATERIAL FROM: TOP NOTCH 3, SECOND EIDTION

GRAMMAR

USING *BE ABLE TO*

PRESENT	**a.** I *am able to touch* my toes. **b.** I *can touch* my toes.	(a) and (b) have basically the same meaning.
FUTURE	**c.** I *will be able to go* shopping tomorrow. **d.** I *can go* shopping tomorrow.	(c) and (d) have basically the same meaning.
PAST	**e.** I *wasn't able to finish* my homework last night. **f.** I *couldn't finish* my homework last night.	(e) and (f) have basically the same meaning.

A *On a separate sheet of paper, make sentences with the same meaning. Use* **be able to**.

1. I can be here tomorrow at ten o'clock.
   → *I'll (I will) be able to be here tomorrow at ten o'clock.*

2. Two students couldn't finish the test.
   → *Two students weren't able to finish the test.*

3. Mark is bilingual. He can speak two languages.

4. Sue can get her own apartment next year.

5. Animals can't speak.

6. Can you touch your toes without bending your knees?

7. Jack couldn't describe the thief.

8. Could you do the homework?

9. I couldn't sleep last night because my apartment was too hot.

10. My roommate can speak four languages. He's multilingual.

11. I'm sorry that I couldn't call you last night.

ABOVE MATERIAL FROM: BASIC ENGLISH GRAMMAR, THIRD EDITION

B *Rewrite each sentence using may, might, or must and be able to.*

1. She has a lot of work to do, so she ___ **might not be able to** ___ keep her doctor's appointment.

2. Dr. Morris isn't in until this afternoon. He _____ see you.

3. I'm sorry, but I have to cancel today. I _____ see you until the end of the week. I'll have to check my schedule.

4. If I leave work at 5:00, I _____ get there by 5:30. It depends on how much traffic there is.

5. Mrs. Graham has called several dentists. She _____ get an appointment for today.

ABOVE MATERIAL FROM: TOP NOTCH 3, SECOND EDITION WORKBOOK

C *On a separate sheet of paper, rewrite each statement, using may (or might) and be able to.*

1. Maybe the doctor can see you tomorrow.

2. Maybe an acupuncturist can help you.

3. Maybe the hotel can recommend a good dentist.

4. Maybe she can't come to the office before 6:00.

5. Maybe you can buy an antihistamine in the hotel gift shop.

ABOVE MATERIAL FROM: TOP NOTCH 3, SECOND EDITION

GRAMMAR

USING *COULD* TO EXPRESS POSSIBILITY

a. — How was the movie? *Could* you *understand* the English? — Not very well. I *could* only *understand* it with the help of subtitles. **b.** — Why isn't Greg in class? — I don't know. He *could be* sick. **c.** Look at those dark clouds. It *could start* raining any minute.	One meaning of *could* is *past ability*, as in (a). Another meaning of *could* is *possibility*. In (b): **He could be sick** has the same meaning as *He may/might be sick*, i.e., *It is possible that he is sick.* In (b): *could* expresses a *present* possibility. In (c): *could* expresses a *future* possibility.

A *Answer each question with* **may, might,** *and* **maybe.** *Include at least three possibilities in each answer. Work in pairs, in small groups, or as a class.*

EXAMPLE: What are you going to do tomorrow?
→ *I don't know. I* **may** *go downtown.* OR *I* **might** *go to the laundromat.*
Maybe *I'll study all day. Who knows?*

1. What are you going to do tomorrow night?

2. What's the weather going to be like tomorrow?

3. What is our teacher going to do tonight?

4. (_____) isn't in class today. Where is he/she?

5. What is your occupation going to be ten years from now?

B 🎧 LISTENING

You will hear sentences with **can, may,** *or* **might.** *Decide if the speakers are expressing ability, possibility, or permission.*

EXAMPLE: You will hear: **A:** Where's Victor?
B: I don't know. He may be sick.

You will choose: ability (possibility) permission

1. ability   possibility   permission

2. ability   possibility   permission

3. ability   possibility   permission

4. ability   possibility   permission

5. ability   possibility   permission

C *Does* **could** *express past, present, or future time? What is the meaning: ability or possibility?*

Sentence	Past	Present	Future	Ability	Possibility
1. I *could be* home late tonight. Don't wait for me for dinner.			×		×
2. Thirty years ago, when he was a small child, David *could speak* Swahili fluently. Now he's forgotten a lot of it.					
3. A: Where's Alicia? **B:** I don't know. She *could be* at the mall.					
4. When I was a child, I *could climb* trees, but now I'm too old.					
5. Let's leave for the airport now. Yuki's plane *could arrive* early, and we want to be there when she arrives.					
6. A: What's that on the carpet? **B:** I don't know. It looks like a bug. Or it *could be* a piece of fuzz.					

ABOVE MATERIAL FROM: **FUNDAMENTALS OF ENGLISH GRAMMAR, FOURTH EDITION**

D *Work in small groups. Look at the pictures of Sandra Diaz and some things that she and her family own. Make guesses about the Diaz family. Give reasons for your guesses.*

EXAMPLE: A: Sandra might be a construction worker. She's wearing a hard hat.

B: Or she could be . . .

C: She couldn't . . .

ABOVE MATERIAL FROM: **FOCUS ON GRAMMAR 3**

E *Suggest possible solutions for each situation. Use* **could.** *Work in pairs, in small groups, or as a class.*

EXAMPLE: Tim has to go to work early tomorrow. His car is completely out of gas. His bicycle is broken.
→ *He could take the bus to work.*
→ *He could get a friend to take him to a gas station to get gas.*
→ *He could try to fix his bike.*
→ *He could get up very early and walk to work. Etc.*

1. Lisa walked to school today. Now she wants to go home. It's raining hard. She doesn't have an umbrella, and she's wearing sandals.

2. Joe and Joan want to get some exercise. They have a date to play tennis this morning, but the tennis court is covered with snow.

3. Roberto just bought a new camera. He has it at home now. He has the instruction manual. It is written in Japanese. He can't read Japanese. He doesn't know how to operate the camera.

4. Albert likes to travel around the world. He is 22 years old. Today he is alone in Paris. He needs to eat, and he needs to find a place to stay overnight. But while he was asleep on the train last night, someone stole his wallet. He has no money.

F 🎧 *Listen to the conversation between a husband and wife. Listen again and complete the sentences with the words you hear.*

In a home office

A: Look at this cord. Do you know what it's for?

B: I don't know. We have so many cords around here with all our electronic equipment. It

_____ for the printer, I guess.
                1

A: No, I checked. The printer isn't missing a cord.

B: It _____ for one of the kid's toys.
            2

A: Yeah, I _____. But they don't have many electronic toys.
              3

B: I have an idea. It _____ for the cell phone. You
                    4

know—the one I had before this one.

A: I bet that's it. We _____ probably throw this out.
                    5

B: Well, let's be sure before we do that.

GRAMMAR

a. I have a very important test tomorrow. I $\left\{ \begin{array}{l} \textit{have to} \\ \textit{have got to} \\ \textit{must} \end{array} \right\}$ *study* tonight.	***Have to***, ***have got to***, and ***must*** have basically the same meaning. They express the idea that something is necessary.
b. I'd like to go with you to the movie this evening, but I can't. I *have to go* to a meeting. **c.** Bye now! I *'ve got to go*. My wife's waiting for me. I'll call you later. **d.** All passengers *must present* their passports at customs upon arrival. **e.** Tommy, you *must hold* onto the railing when you go down the stairs.	***Have to*** is used much more frequently in everyday speech and writing than ***must***. ***Have got to*** is typically used in informal conversation, as in (c). ***Must*** is typically found in written instructions or rules, as in (d). Adults also use it when talking to younger children, as in (e). It sounds very strong.
f. *Do* we *have to bring* pencils to the test? **g.** Why *did* he *have to leave* so early?	QUESTIONS: ***Have to*** is usually used in questions, not ***must*** or ***have got to***. Forms of ***do*** are used with ***have to*** in questions.
h. I *had to study* last night.	The past form of ***have to***, ***have got to***, and ***must*** (meaning necessity) is ***had to***.
i. I *have to* ("hafta") *go* downtown today. **j.** Rita *has to* ("hasta") *go* to the bank. **k.** I've *got to* ("gotta") *study* tonight.	Notice that ***have to***, ***has to***, and ***have got to*** are commonly reduced, as in (i) through (k).
l. I finished all of my homework this afternoon. I *don't have to study* tonight. **m.** Tomorrow is a holiday. Mary *doesn't have to go* to class.	***Don't/doesn't have to*** expresses the idea that something is *not necessary*.
n. Bus passengers *must not talk* to the driver. **o.** Children, you *must not play* with matches!	***Must not*** expresses *prohibition* (DO NOT DO THIS!).
p. You *mustn't play* with matches.	***Must*** + ***not*** = ***mustn't*** (Note: The first "t" is not pronounced.)

A NECESSITY: MUST, HAVE TO, HAVE GOT TO

Choose the correct verb.

1. Last week, John (had to / must) interview five people for the new management position.

2. Professor Drake (had got to / had to) cancel several lectures when she became ill.

3. Why did you (have to / had to) leave work early?

4. I (must / had to) take my daughter to the airport yesterday.

5. Where did John (have to / had to) go for medical help yesterday?

6. We (had to / had got to) contact a lawyer last week about a problem with our neighbors.

7. I (have got to / had to) leave now. I (have to / had to) pick up my kids. They're waiting at school.

8. You (had to / must) have a pencil with an eraser for the exam. Do not bring a pen.

B NECESSITY: MUST, HAVE TO, HAVE GOT TO

Write the past tense of the verbs in italics.

1. I *have to study* for my medical school exams.

    PAST: I _____ **had to study** _____ for my medical school exams.

2. We *have to turn off* our water because of a leak.

    PAST: We _____ our water because of a leak.

3. Do you *have to work* over the holidays?

    PAST: _____ you _____ over the holidays?

4. Jerry *has got to see* the dentist twice this week.

    PAST: Jerry _____ the dentist twice last month.

5. Who *has got to be* in early for work this week?

    PAST: Who _____ in early for work last week?

6. The bank *must close* early today.

    PAST: The bank _____ early yesterday.

GRAMMAR

MAKING LOGICAL CONCLUSIONS: *MUST*

a. **A:** Nancy is yawning. **B:** She *must be* sleepy.	In (a): Speaker B is making a logical guess. He bases his guess on the information that Nancy is yawning. His logical conclusion, his "best guess," is that Nancy is sleepy. He uses *must* to express his logical conclusion.
b. LOGICAL CONCLUSION: Amy plays tennis every day. She *must like* to play tennis. **c.** NECESSITY: If you want to get into the movie theater, you *must buy* a ticket.	COMPARE: ***Must*** can express • a logical conclusion, as in (b). • necessity, as in (c).
d. NEGATIVE LOGICAL CONCLUSION: Eric ate everything on his plate except the pickle. He *must not like* pickles. **e.** PROHIBITION: There are sharks in the ocean near our hotel. We *must not go* swimming there.	COMPARE: ***Must not*** can express • a negative logical conclusion, as in (d). • prohibition, as in (e).

A *Complete the conversations with* **must** *or* **must not.**

1. **A:** Did you offer our guests something to eat?

   B: Yes, but they didn't want anything. They _____**must not**_____ be hungry yet.

2. **A:** You haven't eaten since breakfast? That was hours ago. You _____**must**_____ be hungry.

   B: I am.

3. **A:** Gregory has already had four glasses of water, and now he's having another.

   B: He _____ be really thirsty.

4. **A:** I offered Holly something to drink, but she doesn't want anything.

   B: She _____ be thirsty.

5. **A:** The dog won't eat.

   B: He _____ feel well.

6. **A:** Brian has watery eyes and has been coughing and sneezing.

   B: Poor guy. He _____ have a cold.

ABOVE MATERIAL FROM: FUNDAMENTALS OF ENGLISH GRAMMAR, FOURTH EDITION

B 🎧 *Listen to each conversation and complete the statements. Then listen again to check your answers.*

1. The patient lost _____ when she was eating _____.

2. The patient has _____. She needs to take _____.

    ABOVE MATERIAL FROM: TOP NOTCH 3, SECOND EDITION

3. The patient needs _____ of his _____.

4. The patient would like to try _____ for pain in her _____.

C *Suggest a medication for each person. (Answers will vary.)*

1. _____

2. _____

3. _____

4. _____

5. _____

D *Complete each conversation by drawing your own conclusion with <u>must</u>.*

1. A: I feel really nauseous. I've been vomiting all morning.

    B: You __*must feel terrible*_____.

2. A: My dentist can't fit me in till next month.

    B: Your dentist _____.

3. A: My daughter was sick, but it wasn't anything serious, thank goodness.

    B: You _____.

4. A: My husband fell down and broke his ankle.

    B: He _____!

CONVERSATION MODEL

A 🎧 *Read and listen to someone calling in sick.*

A: I'm afraid I'm not going to be able to come in today.

B: I'm sorry to hear that. Is something wrong?

A: Actually, I'm not feeling too well. I've been coughing and wheezing for a couple of days.

B: That must be awful. Maybe you should see a doctor.

A: I think I will.

B: Good. Call me tomorrow and let me know how you feel. OK?

B 🎧 RHYTHM AND INTONATION

Listen again and repeat. Then practice the Conversation Model with a partner.

C PAIR WORK

Change the Conversation Model to describe other symptoms. Use <u>must</u> or <u>must not</u> to draw conclusions. Then change roles.

A: I'm afraid I'm not going to be able to _____ today.

B: _____. Is something wrong?

A: Actually, I'm not feeling too well. I _____.

B: That must be _____. Maybe you should _____.

A: _____.

B: _____. Call me tomorrow and let me know how you feel. OK?

D CHANGE PARTNERS

Call in sick for other situations such as school or social events.

> **Don't stop!**
> • Ask more questions about your partner's symptoms.
> • Give your partner more suggestions about what to do.

> ♻ **Be sure to recycle this language.**
>
> **Ask questions**
> Are you [coughing]?
> Did you try _____?
> **Make suggestions**
> You should / You'd better _____.
> Why don't you try _____?
> How about _____?
> **Draw conclusions**
> You must feel awful / terrible.
> That must hurt.

ABOVE MATERIAL FROM: TOP NOTCH 3, SECOND EDITION

REVIEW

A *Make logical conclusions with **must** or **must not**. Use the suggested completions and/or your own words.*

1. I am at Cyril's apartment door. I've knocked on the door and have rung the doorbell several times. Nobody has answered the door, *be at home? be out somewhere?*
   → *Cyril must not be at home. He must be out somewhere.*

2. Jennifer reads all the time. She sits in a quiet corner and reads even when people come to visit her. *love books? like books better than people? like to talk to people?*

3. Lara has a full academic schedule, plays on the volleyball team, has the lead in the school play, is a volunteer at the hospital, takes piano lessons, and has a part-time job at an ice-cream store, *be busy all the time? have a lot of spare time? be a hard worker?*

4. Simon gets on the Internet every day as soon as he gets home from work. He stays at his computer until he goes to bed. *be a computer addict? have a happy home life? have a lot of friends?*

ABOVE MATERIAL FROM: FUNDAMENTALS OF ENGLISH GRAMMAR, FOURTH EDITION

B *Look at the pictures. Complete each sentence with* <u>must</u> *or* <u>must not</u> *to draw conclusions.*

1. He _____ be getting a checkup.

2. He _____ be going on vacation.

3. She _____ like the dark.

4. The dog _____ want to go swimming.

5. She _____ have gloves with her.

6. She _____ be feeling well.

C *Circle the word that correctly completes each sentence.*

1. The dentist **may / will** be able to see you today, but I'm not sure.

2. Your gums are really swollen. You **might / must** be in a lot of pain.

3. Bill hates to miss class. He **must / might** be really sick if he's not here today.

4. We **will / might** be able to go shopping this weekend. It depends on if we have time.

5. You lost a filling? That **must / may** really hurt!

6. The patient **might / must** need a blood test. The doctor will have to examine him to be sure.

7. Susan **will / must** be able to meet us for dinner, but she said she'd be a little late.

About Personality

GOALS By the end of Unit 5, you will be able to:

1 Get to know what someone likes.

2 Cheer someone up.

A *Answer the following questions.*

The Psychology of Color

According to research, colors have a powerful effect on us. Take the test and then see if your answers are confirmed by the research. You may be surprised! (Check your answers below.)

1. What color is the most attention-getting?
   ○ black   ○ yellow   ○ red   ○ other

2. What color is most likely to make people feel angry?
   ○ black   ○ yellow   ○ pink   ○ other

3. What color is best for a hospital room?
   ○ pink   ○ white   ○ green   ○ other

4. What color often makes people feel tired?
   ○ green   ○ blue   ○ pink   ○ other

5. What is the least appealing color for food?
   ○ black   ○ yellow   ○ blue   ○ other

What are your color preferences?
Using the colors you know, answer the following.

Write the color you find the most appealing.

_____

Write the color you would most associate with happiness.

_____

Write the color you would most associate with being sad. _____

Answers

1) Experts say red attracts the most attention. Using red for traffic lights and warning lights makes them more noticeable.

2) Studies have shown that being in a yellow room makes it more likely for adults to lose their tempers and for babies to cry.

3) Green is the easiest color on the eye, and it causes people to relax. Painting a hospital room green helps patients get the rest they need.

4) Research has shown that looking at pink can cause people to feel tired. Some sports teams have painted the dressing room of the opposing team pink to reduce the players' energy.

5) Researchers in marketing have found that using blue in processed foods is unappealing. They believe that this is because blue is rare in nature. Painting a restaurant red, on the other hand, increases the appetite. Many restaurants are painted red.

B CLASS SURVEY

Which color was the most popular in your class? Which was the least popular?

C *In your opinion, what makes people like some colors and dislike others?*

"I think people like colors that remind them of things they like."

"I agree. I love blue. It reminds me of the sky. I love being outdoors."

D 🎧 PHOTO STORY

Read and listen to a couple talking about what color to repaint their living room.

Chelsea: You know what? I'm getting a little tired of looking at this wallpaper.
Chad: Well, maybe it's time for a change. What would you think about getting the room painted? I never loved that wallpaper, anyway.
Chelsea: Actually, I don't think either of us did. We only got it because we couldn't agree on a paint color.
Chad: Oh, yeah. Now I remember. You wanted pink and I said it was too feminine.

Chelsea: Actually, I never thought it was pink. To me it was a soft rose.
Chad: Well, what would you say to a nice blue?
Chelsea: Blue? *Way* too masculine.
Chad: *What?!*
Chelsea: I'm just pulling your leg, silly! Blue would be great.

Later that day

Chad: This one's nice—very relaxing.
Chelsea: True, but I'm not sure the furniture would go with it.
Chad: Good point. I'd hate to have to get all new stuff . . . You know, maybe we're on the wrong track.
Chelsea: What do you mean?
Chad: All of a sudden, I'm thinking white. It's classic, and . . .
Chelsea: And it goes with everything!

E PARAPHRASE

Restate the following expressions from the Photo Story in your own way.

1. "I'm just pulling your leg."

2. "I'm not sure the furniture would go with it."

3. "Good point."

4. "Maybe we're on the wrong track."

F *All the following statements are false. Explain how you know they are false.*

1. Chelsea still likes the wallpaper.

> "Chelsea says, 'I'm getting a little tired of looking at this wallpaper.' "

2. Chelsea didn't want a rose-colored living room.

3. Chelsea truly thinks that blue is too masculine.

4. Chelsea thinks the blue Chad likes would go nicely with the furniture.

5. Chad would like to buy new furniture.

6. It's Chelsea's idea to paint the living room white.

7. They agree the furniture wouldn't go with white.

CONVERSATION MODEL

A 🎧 *Read and listen to a conversation about likes and dislikes.*

A: So tell me something about yourself.

B: What would you like to know?

A: Well, for example, what do you like doing in your free time?

B: Let's see. Most of all, I enjoy playing tennis. I find it relaxing. What about you?

A: Well, I find tennis a little boring. But I <u>do</u> love going to the movies.

B: So do I. We should go to the movies together sometime, then.

B 🎧 **RHYTHM AND INTONATION**

Listen again and repeat. Then practice the Conversation Model with a partner.

🎧 **Positive adjectives**
relaxing
enjoyable
exciting

🎧 Negative adjectives
boring
depressing
annoying
scary

C NOTEPADDING

List your likes and dislikes in gerund form. Write a statement with "It's . . ." to say why.

Likes	Dislikes
skiing: It's exciting.	not getting enough sleep: It's awful.

Likes	Dislikes

D PAIR WORK

Using your notepad, personalize the Conversation Model. Include gerund and infinitive direct objects. Ask about other times and occasions.

A: So tell me something about yourself.

B: What would you like to know?

A: Well, for example, what do you like doing _____?

B: Let's see. Most of all, I enjoy _____. I find it _____. What about you?

A: Well, I _____.

B: _____.

Other times and occasions
- on weekends
- on vacations
- with your friends / family
- for lunch / dinner

E CHANGE PARTNERS

Talk about other likes and dislikes.

Don't stop!

Ask about your partner's plans for this weekend. Use the following verbs with direct object infinitives:

need	want
plan	would like

For example:
"What do you **plan to do** this weekend?"

ABOVE MATERIAL FROM: TOP NOTCH 2, SECOND EDITION

GRAMMAR

VERB + GERUND

VERB GERUND **a.** I *enjoy walking* in the park.	A gerund is the *-ing* form of a verb. It is used as a noun. In (a): ***walking*** is a gerund. It is used as the object of the verb ***enjoy.***

Common Verbs Followed by Gerunds
enjoy   **b.** I *enjoy working* in my garden.
finish   **c.** Ann *finished studying* at midnight.
quit   **d.** David *quit smoking*.
mind   **e.** Would you *mind opening* the window?
postpone   **f.** I *postponed doing* my homework.
put off   **g.** I *put off doing* my homework.
keep (on) **h.** *Keep (on) working*. Don't stop.
consider   **i.** I*'m considering going* to Hawaii.
think about **j.** I*'m thinking about going* to Hawaii.
discuss   **k.** They *discussed getting* a new car.
talk about **l.** They *talked about getting* a new car.
	The verbs in the list are followed by gerunds. The list also contains phrasal verbs (e.g., *put off*) that are followed by gerunds.
	The verbs in the list are NOT followed by *to* + the simple form of a verb (an infinitive).
	  INCORRECT: *I enjoy to walk in the park.*
	  INCORRECT: *Bob finished to study.*
	  INCORRECT: *I'm thinking to go to Hawaii.*

m. I *considered not going* to class.	Negative form: ***not*** + *gerund*

A *Complete each sentence with the correct form of a verb from the list.*

clean	hand in	sleep
close	hire	smoke
eat	pay	work

1. The Boyds own a bakery. They work seven days a week and they are very tired. They are thinking about . . .

   a. _____ fewer hours a day.

   b. _____ their shop for a few weeks and going on vacation.

   c. _____ more workers for their shop.

2. Joseph wants to live a healthier life. He made several New Year's resolutions. For example, he has quit . . .

   a. _____ cigars

   b. _____ high-fat foods.

   c. _____ until noon on weekends.

3. Martina is a procrastinator.* She puts off . . .

   a. _____ her bills.

   b. _____ her assignments to her teacher.

   c. _____ her apartment.

*procrastinator = someone who postpones or delays doing things

B *Complete each sentence with a gerund.*

1. We discussed _____*going/driving*_____ to the ocean for our vacation.

2. The Porters' car is too small for their growing family. They're considering _____ a bigger one.

3. When Martha finished _____ the floor, she dusted the furniture.

4. Beth doesn't like her job. She's talking about _____ a different job.

5. **A:** Are you listening to me?

   B: Yes. Keep _____. I'm listening.

6. **A:** Do you want to take a break?

   B: No. I'm not tired yet. Let's keep on _____ for another hour or so.

7. **A:** Would you mind _____ the window?

   B: No problem. I'm too hot, too.

C 🎧 *Complete each conversation with the words you hear. Note: There is a gerund in each completion.*

EXAMPLE: You will hear:　　**A:** I enjoy watching sports on TV, especially soccer.
　　　　　　　　　　　　B: Me too.

　　　　　　　You will write:　_____*enjoy watching*_____

1. **A:** When you _____ your homework, could you help me in the kitchen?

   B: Sure.

2. **A:** Do you have any plans for this weekend?

   B: Henry and I _____ the dinosaur exhibit at the museum.

3. **A:** I didn't understand the answer. _____ it?

   B: I'd be happy to.

4. **A:** I'm _____ the meeting tomorrow.

   B: Really? Why? I hope you go. We need your input.

5. **A:** I've been working on this math problem for the last half hour, and I still don't understand it.

   B: Well, don't give up. _____.

　　　　　　　ABOVE MATERIAL FROM: FUNDAMENTALS OF ENGLISH GRAMMAR, FOURTH EDITION

D *Complete each sentence with the correct form of a verb from the list. The first one is done for you.*

✓bake	drive	get	paint	smoke	turn down
do	find	move	run	take	

1. I always enjoy _____ **baking** _____ bread.

2. Would you mind _____ the stereo? I'm trying to sleep.

3. Hiro put off _____ his homework all week. Now he is too tired to do it.

4. My husband and I are thinking about _____ a puppy, but we're not sure yet.

5. Will took a wrong turn on the road, but he kept _____ because he didn't want his girlfriend to know he had made a mistake.

6. We finished _____ our apartment. Now we can decorate the walls.

7. The Davisons have discussed _____ closer to the city so Mr. Davison would have a shorter commute to work.

8. When did Viktor quit _____? He looks much healthier than the last time I saw him.

9. Every year we consider _____ a trip to Asia, but we haven't done it yet.

10. We are going to postpone _____ a meeting room until we know how many people will attend.

11. Katarina and Liz are talking about _____ in the city marathon next year.

ABOVE MATERIAL FROM: FUNDAMENTALS OF ENGLISH GRAMMAR, 4TH ED TEST BANK

GRAMMAR

VERB + INFINITIVE

a. Tom *offered to lend* me some money. **b.** I've *decided to buy* a new car.	Some verbs are followed by an infinitive. Infinitive = *to* + *the simple form of a verb*
c. I've *decided not to keep* my old car.	Negative form: *not* + *infinitive*

Common Verbs Followed by Infinitives

want	hope	decide	seem	learn (how)
need	expect	promise	appear	try
would like	plan	offer	pretend	
would love	intend	agree	suggest	(can't) afford
	mean	refuse	practice	(can't) wait
			choose	(can't) stand

A *Complete Lucia's letter. Use gerunds and infinitives. Remember to put the verbs in the correct tense.*

Hi Rebecca,

Well, I finally made a change! Last week I said to myself, "I _____ at our old
                                                         1. can't stand / look

kitchen walls one more day!" So I _____ them! My roommate Sara said we should
                                        2. decide / repaint

_____ a plan before we do it. She even _____ a month or
  3. discuss / make   4. suggest / take

two to think about it. She said we should _____ first, but I already know how to
                                     5. practice / paint

paint. I don't _____. Anyway, I _____ new things. Finally,
            6. need / learn   7. not mind / try

we _____ the kitchen a cheerful color—bright yellow! I'm not sure, but Sara
      8. choose / give

_____ the new color. In fact, I don't think she _____! But I hope
  9. not seem / like   10. enjoy / paint

she does, because I _____ the living room next. I _____ it tomato
          11. plan / paint   12. would like / paint

red! What do you think about that?

Lucia

Verb + Gerund or Infinitive

B *Choose the correct answer. In some cases, both answers are correct.*

EXAMPLE: Pat hates _____ sad movies.
    (**a.**) to watch   (**b.**) watching

1. Stan offered _____ Christopher with his math.
  a. to help   **b.** helping

2. In the mountains, it continued _____ for a week.
  a. to snow   **b.** snowing

3. We have some free time before dinner. Let's go _____.
  a. to sightsee   **b.** sightseeing

4. From a distance, the bear appeared _____ smaller than he was.
  a. to be   **b.** being

5. Have you thought about _____ extra employees for the holiday season?

    a. to hire   **b.** hiring

6. Miroslav and Ivana have decided _____ at the same company.

    a. to work   **b.** working

7. Pierre began _____ English six months ago.

    a. to study   **b.** studying

8. Mrs. Allen can't stand _____ in icy weather.

    a. to drive   **b.** driving

9. We can't wait _____ our cousins on the coast.

    a. to visit   **b.** visiting

10. Bobby learned how _____ a computer when he was five years old.

    a. to use   **b.** using

ABOVE MATERIAL FROM: FUNDAMENTALS OF ENGLISH GRAMMAR, FOURTH EDITION TEST BANK

GRAMMAR

Gerunds and infinitives as direct objects

Remember two other -ing forms:
She is **painting.** (present participle)
The trip was **relaxing.** (participial adjective)

Gerunds and infinitives come from verb forms but function as nouns. A gerund or an infinitive can be a direct object of a verb.

    Gerund = an -ing form of a verb
    She enjoys painting.

    Infinitive = to + a base form
    He wants to paint the kitchen yellow.

Use a gerund after the following verbs: avoid, can't stand, discuss, dislike, don't mind, enjoy, feel like, practice, quit, suggest

Use an infinitive after the following verbs: agree, be sure, choose, decide, expect, hope, learn, need, plan, seem, want, wish, would like

Other verbs can be followed by either a gerund or an infinitive: begin, continue, hate, like, love, prefer, start

A GRAMMAR PRACTICE

Complete the advice about managing feelings, using the verbs plus gerund or infinitive direct objects.

Feeling blue? Then take care of yourself!

Everybody feels a little sad from time to time. If you _____
(1. not feel like / talk)

about what is making you unhappy and you _____ advice
(2. dislike / read)

books, here are some helpful hints. First of all, _____
(3. decide / take care of)

your health. _____ coffee and alcohol. Coffee espe-
(4. Avoid / drink)

cially can make you feel nervous, but exercise can reduce nervousness and

calm you. If you _____, I _____ with
(5 choose / exercise).   (6. suggest / go)

a friend you _____ time with. _____ right and, importantly,
(7. enjoy / spend)   (8. Be sure / eat)

_____ lots of sleep. If you _____ a day off from work and you
(9. be sure / get)   (10. would like / take)

_____ to the movies or _____ a walk in the park, just do it. Every-
(11. want / go)   (12. plan / take)

body needs to take a break sometimes. And when life gets too depressing, _____ your-
(13. learn / cheer)

self up. You can be your own best friend! Oh, and a final note: Everybody finds certain colors "happy."

Try to wear the colors *you* find most cheerful.

PRONUNCIATION

B 🎧 REDUCTION OF <u>TO</u> IN INFINITIVES

Notice how an unstressed <u>to</u> reduces to /tə/. Read and listen. Then listen again and repeat.

1. I decided to repaint the bedroom a happier color.

2. We plan to see the World Cup Finals.

3. She doesn't like to hear people talking on cell phones.

4. I know you'd like to choose a more cheerful color.

ABOVE MATERIAL FROM: TOP NOTCH 2, SECOND EDITION

C *Complete each sentence with a gerund or infinitive and an adjective from the box.*

| annoying | boring | depressing | enjoyable | exciting | relaxing |

1. I've had the most stressful week at work! I need _____ a massage this weekend.

get

   I find it so _____.

2. We don't want _____ tonight's game. Our favorite team is in the championship.

miss

   It's going to be really _____!

3. Most kids hate _____ shopping. They think it's not any fun and complain, "This is

go

   so _____."

4. I had to ask a classmate to please quit _____ his pencil on the desk. I found it very

tap

   _____.

5. I don't feel like _____ that film. I hear it's very _____. I'm not in

watch

   the mood for a sad movie.

6. Max usually doesn't mind _____. He finds it pretty _____.

exercise

D *Write about your plans for the weekend. Use verbs with direct object infinitives, such as <u>need</u>, <u>plan</u>, <u>want</u>, and <u>would like</u>.*

E *Complete each sentence with the correct form of a word from the list.*

be	fly to	hear	lend	visit
buy	get to	hurt	see	watch
eat	go to	leave	tell	

1. I'm planning _____ *to fly to/to go to* _____ Chicago next week.

2. Hasan promised not _____ late for the wedding.

3. My husband and I would love _____ Fiji.

4. What time do you expect _____ Chicago?

5. You seem _____ in a good mood today.

6. Nadia appeared _____ asleep, but she wasn't. She was only pretending.

7. Nadia pretended _____ asleep. She pretended not

   _____ me when I spoke to her.

8. The Millers can't afford _____ a house.

9. My friend offered _____ me some money.

10. Tommy doesn't like broccoli. He refuses _____ it.

11. My wife and I wanted to do different things this weekend. Finally, I agreed

    _____ a movie with her Saturday, and she agreed

    _____ the football game with me on Sunday.

broccoli

12. I try _____ class on time every day.

13. I can't wait _____ my family again! It's been a long time.

14. I'm sorry. I didn't mean _____ you.

15. I learned how _____ time when I was six.

F *Choose the correct verbs.*

1. It started _____ around midnight.
   a. snow   **b.** snowing   **c.** to snow

2. I continued _____ even though everyone else stopped.
   a. work   **b.** working   **c.** to work

3. I like _____ emails from my friends.
   a. get   **b.** getting   **c.** to get

4. I would like _____ an email from my son who's away at college.
   a. get   **b.** getting   **c.** to get

   ABOVE MATERIAL FROM: FUNDAMENTALS OF ENGLISH GRAMMAR, FOURTH EDITION

5. I love _____ to baseball games.

    a. go   **b.** going   **c.** to go

6. I would love _____ to the baseball game tomorrow.

    a. go   **b.** going   **c.** to go

7. I hate _____ to pushy salespeople.

    a. talk   **b.** talking   **c.** to talk

8. I can't stand _____ in long lines.

    a. wait   **b.** waiting   **c.** to wait

ABOVE MATERIAL FROM: FUNDAMENTALS OF ENGLISH GRAMMAR, FOURTH EDITION

CONVERSATION MODEL

A 🎧 *Read and listen to someone trying to cheer a friend up.*

A: You look down. What's up?

B: Oh, nothing serious. I'm just tired of the same old grind. But thanks for asking.

A: I know what you mean. I'm tired of working, too. How about going to a movie?

B: Great idea. Let's go!

B 🎧 RHYTHM AND INTONATION

Listen again and repeat. Then practice the Conversation Model with a partner.

GRAMMAR

Gerunds as objects of prepositions

A gerund (-ing form of a verb) can function as an object of a preposition.

	preposition	object
I'm afraid	**of**	**flying**.
She's bored	**with**	**cooking**.
She objects	**to**	**discussing** her feelings.

Be careful! Don't use an infinitive as the object of a preposition. Don't say: Let's go to a movie instead ~~of to watch~~ TV.

Expressions followed by gerunds

Adjective + preposition

angry about	afraid of
excited about	sick / tired of
depressed about	bored with
happy / sad about	

Verb + preposition

complain about	apologize for
talk about	believe in
worry about	object to
think about	

ABOVE MATERIAL FROM: TOP NOTCH 2, SECOND EDITION

A GRAMMAR PRACTICE

Complete the descriptions with prepositions and gerunds.

Ted

Ted is an extrovert. Like most extroverts, he's direct. And he's honest; he believes _____ the truth to everyone.

At his job, he works with other people and he never complains _____ long hours. He works hard and doesn't worry _____ work on weekends or holidays.

He has a few fears, though. Most of all, he's afraid _____.

1 tell
2 work
3 have to
4 fly

Nicole

Ted's wife, Nicole, on the other hand, is an introvert. But she doesn't object _____ about herself from time to time.

Right now, she's bored _____ a student, and she's sick and tired _____ so many long reports and _____ exams every few weeks! She's angry _____ spend so much time in front of a computer.

However, unlike Ted, she's not at all afraid _____! She's excited _____ on vacation.

5 talk
6 be
7 write
8 take
9 have to
10 fly
11 go

B PAIR WORK

Answer the questions about yourself, using gerunds. Then share the information with a partner.

> "Right now, I'm happy about getting engaged!"

Right now, what are you . . .	
happy about?	
excited about?	
bored with?	
sick and tired of?	

C NOTEPADDING

Make a list of things that you are tired of. Write them as gerunds.

What are you tired of?
studying so hard

♻ **Be sure to recycle this language.**

Be sure to (get enough sleep).
You'd better start (eating healthier food).
You should think about (quitting your job).
What about (spending the weekend at a spa)?
How about (getting a pedicure)?
That always helps me.
That's a good idea.
I'll think about that.

Don't stop!
Make more suggestions.
Use gerunds and infinitives.

D PAIR WORK

Role-play cheering someone up. Use your partner's list for ideas. Then change roles.

A: You look down. What's up?

B: Oh, nothing serious. I'm just tired of _____.
But thanks for asking.

A: I know what you mean. _____.

B: _____.

E CHANGE PARTNERS

Cheer your new partner up.

F *Complete the conversation. Use the correct preposition with the verb or adjective, and a gerund.*

A: You look a little blue. What's up?

B: Oh, nothing really. I'm just ___sick of working___ late every night.
    1. sick / work

A: Is that all? You look really down.

B: I'm _____ the same thing every day. And I also feel _____ too little time
    2. bored / do   3. sad / spend

at home.

A: Have you _____ overtime?
    4. complained / work

B: No. I'm _____ my boss angry. I had to _____ a report late. And now my
    5. afraid / make   6. apologize / finish

boss is _____ us more work.
    7. talking / give

A: Wow! I see why you are feeling blue. Why don't you start looking for a new job?

B: Maybe I should.

ABOVE MATERIAL FROM: TOP NOTCH 2, SECOND EDITION WORKBOOK

GRAMMAR

A WARM-UP

Read the passage and then agree or disagree with the statements.

A White Lie

Jane gave her friend Lisa a book for her birthday. When Lisa opened it, she tried to look excited, but her husband had already given her the same book. Lisa had just finished reading it, but she thanked Jane and said she was looking forward to reading it. Lisa told a "white lie." White lies are minor or unimportant lies that a person often tells to avoid hurting someone else's feelings.

1. Telling white lies is common.   yes   no

2. It is sometimes acceptable to tell a white lie.   yes   no

3. I sometimes tell white lies.   yes   no

ABOVE MATERIAL FROM: FUNDAMENTALS OF ENGLISH GRAMMAR, FOURTH EDITION

USING GERUNDS AS SUBJECTS; USING IT + INFINITIVE

a. *Riding horses* is fun. **b.** *It* is fun *to ride* horses. **c.** *Coming to class on time* is important. **d.** *It* is important *to come to class on time*.	Examples (a) and (b) have the same meaning. In (a): A gerund (**riding**) is the subject of the sentence. Notice: The verb (is) is singular because a gerund is singular.* In (b): **It** is used as the subject of the sentence. **It** has the same meaning as the infinitive phrase at the end of the sentence: **it** means **to ride horses**.

*It is also correct (but less common) to use an infinitive as the subject of a sentence: *To ride horses is fun.*

B GRAMMAR AND SPEAKING: PAIRWORK

Make sentences with the same meaning as the given sentences, and then decide if you agree with them. Circle yes or no. Share your answers with a partner.

Living in this town

Part I. Use a gerund as the subject.

1. It's hard to meet people here.
   → *Meeting people here is hard.*   yes   no

2. It takes time to make friends here.   yes   no

3. It is easy to get around the town.   yes   no

4. Is it expensive to live here?   yes   no

Part II. Use **it** + *an infinitive.*

5. Finding things to do on weekends is hard.
   → *It's hard to find things to do on weekends.*   yes   no

6. Walking alone at night is dangerous.   yes   no

7. Exploring this town is fun.   yes   no

8. Is finding affordable housing difficult?   yes   no

C LET'S TALK: INTERVIEW

Interview your classmates. Ask a question and then agree or disagree with your classmate's answer. Practice using both gerunds and infinitives in your answers.

EXAMPLE:

SPEAKER A *(book open):*   Which is easier: to make money or to spend money?
SPEAKER B *(book closed):*   It's easier to spend money than (it is) to make money.
SPEAKER A *(book open):*   I agree. Spending money is easier than making money. OR
                            I don't agree. I think that making money is easier than
                            spending money.

1. Which is more fun: to visit a big city or to spend time in the countryside?

2. Which is more difficult: to write English or to read English?

3. Which is easier: to understand spoken English or to speak it?

4. Which is more expensive: to go to a movie or to go to a concert?

5. Which is more comfortable: to wear shoes or to go barefoot?

6. Which is more satisfying: to give gifts or to receive them?

7. Which is more dangerous: to ride in a car or to ride in an airplane?

8. Which is more important: to come to class on time or to get an extra hour of sleep in the morning?

GRAMMAR

A WARM-UP

Agree or disagree with these statements.

In my culture . . .

1. it is common for people to shake hands when they meet.   yes   no

2. it is important for people to look one another in the eye when they are introduced.   yes   no

3. it is strange for people to kiss one another on the cheek when they meet.   yes   no

IT + INFINITIVE: USING FOR (SOMEONE)

a. *You* should *study* hard. **b.** It is important *for you* to study hard. **c.** *Mary* should study hard. **d.** It is important *for Mary* to study hard. **e.** *We* don't have to go to the meeting. **f.** It isn't necessary *for us* to go to the meeting. **g.** *A dog* can't talk. **h.** It is impossible *for a dog* to talk.	Examples (a) and (b) have a similar meaning. Notice the pattern in (b): ***It is*** + *adjective* + ***for*** (someone) + *infinitive phrase*

B LOOKING AT GRAMMAR

Complete the sentences with the given information. Use for (someone) and an infinitive phrase in each completion.

1. Students should do their homework.

   It's really important _____ *for students to do their homework* _____.

2. Teachers should speak clearly.

   It's very important _____.

3. We don't have to hurry. There's plenty of time.

   It isn't necessary _____.

4. A fish can't live out of water for more than a few minutes.

   It's impossible _____.

5. Working parents have to budget their time carefully.

   It's necessary _____.

6. A young child usually can't sit still for a long time.

   It's difficult _____.

7. My family spends birthdays together.

   It's traditional _____.

8. My brother would love to travel to Mars someday.

   Will it be possible _____ to Mars someday?

9. I usually can't understand Mr. Alvarez. He talks too fast. How about you?

   Is it easy _____?

C LET'S TALK

Work in small groups. Make sentences by combining the given ideas with the words in the list. Use gerunds as subjects or **it** *+ an infinitive. Share some of your sentences for other groups to agree or disagree with.*

boring	embarrassing	hard	impossible	scary
dangerous	exciting	illegal	interesting	waste of time
educational	fun	important	relaxing	

EXAMPLE: ride a bicycle
→ *Riding a bicycle is fun.* OR *It's fun to ride a bicycle.*

1. ride a roller coaster

2. read newspapers

3. study economics

4. drive five miles over the speed limit

5. walk in a cemetery at night

6. know the meaning of every word in a dictionary

7. never tell a lie

8. visit museums

ABOVE MATERIAL FROM: **FUNDAMENTALS OF ENGLISH GRAMMAR, FOURTH EDITION**

D GERUND AS SUBJECT; *IT* + INFINITIVE

Complete the sentences by using a gerund as the subject or **it** *+ infinitive. Add* **is** *where appropriate. Use the verbs in the list.*

complete	eat	live
drive	✓learn	swim

1. a. _____It is_____ easy for anyone _____to learn_____ how to cook an egg.

   b. _____Learning_____ how to cook an egg _____is_____ easy for anyone.

2. a. _____ nutritious food _____ important for your health.

   b. _____ important for your health _____ nutritious food.

3. a. _____ on the wrong side of the road _____ against the law.

   b. _____ against the law _____ on the wrong side of the road.

4. a. _____ fun for both children and adults _____ in the warm sea.

   b. _____ in the warm sea _____ fun for both children and adults.

 ABOVE MATERIAL FROM: **FUNDAMENTALS OF ENGLISH GRAMMAR, 4TH ED WORKBOOK**

5. **a.** _____ expensive _____ in a dormitory?

b. _____ in a dormitory expensive?

6. **a.** _____ difficult _____ these sentences correctly?

b. _____ these sentences correctly difficult?

E PURPOSE: TO VS. FOR

Rewrite the sentences. Use **it** *. . . for someone + an infinitive phrase.* *Use the adjective in parentheses.*

1. Shy people have a hard time meeting others at social events. (*difficult*)

_____ **It is difficult for shy people to meet** _____ others at social events.

2. In many cultures, young children sleep in the same room as their parents. (*customary*)

In many cultures, _____ in the same room as their parents.

3. Airline pilots need to have good eyesight. (*necessary*)

_____ good eyesight.

4. Many teenagers can't wake up early. (*hard*)

_____ early.

5. Elderly people need to keep their minds active. (*important*)

_____ their minds active.

6. People don't like listening to monotone speakers. (*boring*)

_____ to monotone speakers.

7. Scientists will never know the origin of every disease in the world. (*impossible*)

_____ the origin of every disease in the world.

Culture and Commerce

GOALS By the end of Unit 6, you will be able to:

1 Discuss the relationship between culture and commerce.

2 Make predictions about the future.

A *Discuss the questions with the class.*

1. Look at the photo. Why do you think these women are wearing coils around their necks?

2. Read the title of the unit. *Commerce* means business. In your opinion, what is the relationship between culture and commerce in tourism?

B *Work in a small group. First, read each statement and decide your opinion. Write* **SD** *(strongly disagree),* **D** *(disagree),* **A** *(agree), or* **SA** *(strongly agree) in each blank. Then discuss your opinions with the group.*

Long-necked women from the Pa Daung tribe in Thailand, wearing brass coils around their necks

_____ 1. Tourism can be harmful to people living in a tourist community.

_____ 2. Tourism can help people have a better life.

_____ 3. Tourist activities that harm people or the environment should not be allowed.

_____ 4. Any tourist activity that makes money should be allowed.

_____ 5. Tourism is a good way for people to make money.

_____ 6. Tourism destroys the natural environment.

BACKGROUND AND VOCABULARY

A 🎧 *A travel blog (web log) is an Internet site where people write about their trips. Read and listen to the* **travel blog about a trip to Thailand.**

Travel Blog: Northern Thailand

We've had a great time exploring Northern Thailand so far. It's really interesting and there's so much to see!

One thing I've learned is that elephants are the national symbol of Thailand. They are very important in Thai history and cultural **(1) traditions**. Elephants are also a big tourist **(2) attraction**, so there are many different elephant parks for tourists to visit. We decided to visit one, but we soon found out that there is a lot of **(3) controversy** about them. Some parks treat the elephants very badly. They are not treated with respect and have to perform **(4) degrading** tricks for tourists, like playing basketball and dancing. The owners don't really care about the elephants; they just want to **(5) make a living** by showing the animals to tourists.

However, the elephant park we went to is very different. In this place, they are trying to **(6) preserve** the wild elephant population. It's a large, beautiful park where the elephants can walk around freely. They are so playful! I took this photo of two young elephants walking together with their trunks **(7) wrapped** around each other, just like two kids walking hand-in-hand. Going to the park was an amazing experience, much better than seeing elephants in a **(8) zoo**. I also bought some nice **(9) souvenirs**: a stuffed elephant toy for my niece and a carved wooden elephant for my parents.

Tomorrow we're going to see another unusual sight: the village of Nai Soi where the long-necked women of the Pa Daung tribe live. The women wear brass coils to **(10) stretch** their necks. More on that tomorrow!

B *Write the number of each boldfaced word or phrase in the text next to its definition.*

_____ **a.** disagreement among people

_____ **b.** a place where animals are kept so that people can look at them

_____ **c.** to keep something from being changed or harmed

_____ **d.** customs (special activities) that have existed for a long time

_____ **e.** things you buy to help you remember a place

_____ **f.** to make something longer by pulling it

_____ **g.** folded around something

_____ **h.** showing no respect

_____ **i.** something interesting to see or do

_____ **j.** to earn money from

FOCUS ON LISTENING

LISTENING ONE: Tourist Attraction or Human Zoo?

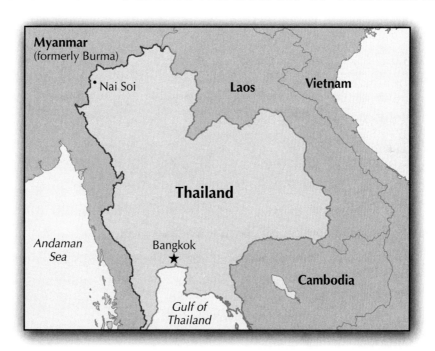

A 🎧 *You will hear a news report about the village of the long-necked women in Thailand. Listen to this excerpt from the report. Circle your prediction.*

This news report will present the tourist attraction in _____.
   a. a positive way
   b. a negative way
   c. a way that is both positive and negative

B 🎧 LISTEN FOR MAIN IDEAS

*Listen to the radio news report. Write **T** (true) or **F** (false) for each statement.*

The tradition of the long-necked women . . .

_____ 1. started in Thailand.

_____ 2. brings tourists to the village to buy souvenirs and take pictures.

_____ 3. allows women to earn money for their families.

_____ 4. is safe and healthy for the women.

_____ 5. has caused controversy among tourists.

_____ 6. will continue as long as tourists keep coming.

C 🎧 LISTEN FOR DETAILS

Listen again. Circle the best answer to complete each statement.

1. About _____ tourists visit the long-necked women every year.
   a. 1,000
   b. 10,000
   c. 100,000

2. When they lived in Myanmar, the Pa Daung _____.
   a. sold souvenirs to tourists
   b. fought in a war
   c. were farmers

3. A full set of brass coils _____.
   a. weighs up to 22 pounds
   b. costs up to $22
   c. takes up to 22 years to put on

4. A long-necked woman cannot remove the coils because _____.
   a. her neck is very weak
   b. she won't make any money
   c. her family won't let her

5. Back in Myanmar, the tradition of stretching women's necks _____.
   a. has almost disappeared
   b. is still strong
   c. is becoming more popular

6. A long-necked woman can make $70 to $80 _____ from tourists.
   a. a week
   b. a month
   c. a year

7. Sandra feels that she is helping the Pa Daung women because she is _____.
   a. spending money in the village
   b. not visiting the village
   c. bringing food to the village

8. Fredrick uses the image of _____ to describe the Pa Daung women.
   a. animals in a zoo
   b. prisoners in jail
   c. actors in a show

D 🎧 MAKE INFERENCES

Listen to excerpts from the report. Choose adjectives from the list to describe the speaker's tone of voice and take notes on word choices. Then decide whether the person would agree or disagree with the statement.

accepting	argumentative	confused	frustrated	lucky
angry	confident	contented	homesick	sad

Excerpt One: *Pa Peiy*

Tone of voice: <u>*sad, accepting*</u>

Word choice: <u>*OK = not great*</u>

Pa Peiy would (agree / (disagree)) with the statement:

"I like wearing the neck coils."

Excerpt Two: *Ma Nang*

Tone of voice: _____

Word choice: _____

Ma Nang would (agree / disagree) with the statement:

"I'm happy that the tourists come to look at me."

Excerpt Three: *Sandra*

Tone of voice: _____

Word choice: _____

Sandra would (agree / disagree) with the statement:

"I'm worried about how tourism affects the Pa Daung."

Excerpt Four: *Fredrick*

Tone of voice: _____

Word choice: _____

Fredrick would (agree / disagree) with the statement:

"I don't like the tradition of neck stretching."

E *Discuss the statements in a small group. Do you agree or disagree? Explain your opinions.*

1. I would like to visit the women of the Pa Daung tribe.

2. The Pa Daung women are helped by the tourism in their village.

LISTENING TWO: Town Hall Meeting in Cape Cod

A *Look at the information about Cape Cod. What can you conclude about this tourist destination?*

CAPE COD, MASSACHUSETTS

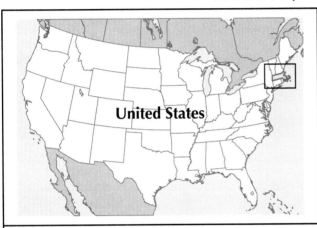 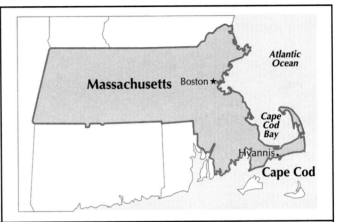

Cape Cod is one of New England's most popular tourist attractions, with more than 5 million tourists visiting each year. During the summer season, from June to September, tourists come to relax at the beach, shop in the small towns, and eat fresh seafood. During the rest of the year, the population drops to about 200,000. Many summer businesses, such as restaurants and souvenir shops, close for the winter.

B 🎧 *Listening Two is an excerpt from a town hall meeting. The mayor (the town leader) is leading the meeting. The townspeople are listening and expressing their opinions. Listen and circle the best answer to complete each sentence. Compare your answers with a partner's.*

1. The traffic on Cape Cod _____.
   a. gets worse during the summer
   b. is bad all year
   c. is better now that there are buses

2. _____ is difficult to find on Cape Cod.
   a. Low-priced housing
   b. Housing for families
   c. Vacation housing

3. The restaurant owner knows a waitress who lives _____.
   a. in her car
   b. far from her work
   c. in a hotel

4. The woman who runs the souvenir shop says _____.
   a. she plans to open another store next year in a neighboring village
   b. she does most of her business during the summer
   c. her business is doing badly this year

5. The business owner says he lost money because _____.
   a. too many stores are selling the same things
   b. tourists go to the beach instead of going shopping
   c. the rainy weather kept tourists away

INTEGRATE LISTENINGS: One and Two

STEP 1: ORGANIZE

A *Work with a partner. In the chart, write the positive and negative effects of tourism on the Pa Daung tribe and the Cape Cod residents.*

EFFECTS OF TOURISM

	Positive Effects	**Negative Effects**
Pa Daung Tribe		Women continue to wrap their necks.
Cape Cod Residents	Tourists spend money.	

B *Draw a circle around the effects that are similar in both communities.*

STEP 2: SYNTHESIZE

With your partner, debate the topic "Does tourism help or hurt people in tourist communities?"

STUDENT A: take the pro position (Tourism has positive effects on people in tourist communities).
STUDENT B: take the con position (Tourism has negative effects on people in tourist communities).

Each person has two to three minutes to present his or her position. Use the information from Step 1 to support your position. Then switch partners.

Useful Language

- I think tourism helps / hurts tourist communities because . . .

- For example, in Thailand / Cape Cod . . .

- One tourist / Pa Daung woman / Cape Cod resident said . . .

- Also . . .

- Another argument for / against tourism is . . .

Focus on Speaking

VOCABULARY

A Review

Cross out the word that doesn't belong in each group. Consult a dictionary if necessary.

EXAMPLE

zoo	~~museum~~	animal park	wildlife center
1. afford	have money for	pay for	borrow from
2. controversy	argument	debate	agreement
3. depend on	rely on	need	choose
4. degrading	polite	embarrassing	painful
5. make a living	earn money	enjoy life	get paid
6. preserve	destroy	save	care for
7. season	days of the week	time of year	period of time
8. souvenir	reminder	keepsake	equipment
9. stretch	enlarge	make longer	reduce
10. tourist attraction	place to see	guidebook	point of interest
11. tradition	habit	change	belief
12. village	small town	community	city
13. wrap	open	cover	surround

B Expand

Read the letter to the editor about the effects of tourism in Cape Cod.

TO THE EDITOR:
Effects of Tourism

Millions of tourists visit Cape Cod each year. Most tourists come here to relax at the beach and enjoy our delicious seafood. Others like to **get off the beaten path** and explore parts of the Cape that most tourists don't see. Whatever they do here, we appreciate the tourists because most **locals** have jobs that depend on tourism, such as shop owners and restaurant workers.

However, tourism can also have a negative **impact** on the area. The cost of housing is one example. The cost of housing keeps increasing, so many families can't afford to buy a home. **In the long run**, this problem

ABOVE MATERIAL FROM: NORTHSTAR LEVEL 3, THIRD EDITION

will force families to leave the Cape and live elsewhere.

Problems like this affect our **way of life** here on the Cape. Life is becoming more difficult for the year-round residents.

We need to **find a compromise** that will preserve the tourist income for the area and allow the locals to continue living here.

Michelle Connelly
Sandwich, Mass.

Match the words and phrases on the left with the definitions on the right.

_____ **1.** get off the beaten path

_____ **2.** locals

_____ **3.** impact

_____ **4.** in the long run

_____ **5.** way of life

_____ **6.** find a compromise

a. the effect of a situation

b. customs and habits of daily living

c. far in the future

d. go somewhere that most tourists don't visit

e. look for ideas that two groups of people can share

f. people who live in a particular place

C CREATE

Work in a small group. Each person thinks of a tourist destination he or she has visited. Take turns making a short presentation about the destination. Answer the questions in your presentation. Use the vocabulary from the box.

1. What tourist destination did you visit?

2. What are the major tourist attractions?

3. What impact does tourism have on the locals?

4. What impact does tourism have on the environment?

afford	find a compromise	preserve
controversial	get off the beaten path	season
degrading	in the long run	souvenir
depend on	locals	way of life
	make a living	

GRAMMAR

A *Work with a partner. Read the conversation between two residents of Cape Cod. Then switch roles and repeat.*

A: Did you see the weather report today? They say it**'ll** keep raining all week.

B: Really? That's bad. **If it keeps raining**, the tourists **won't** come. They**'ll** stay home.

A: I know. I**'ll probably** lose money this week.

FUTURE PREDICTIONS WITH *IF*-CLAUSES

1. Use *will* + base form and *will not* (*won't*) + base form to make predictions about the future. *Will* is usually contracted in speech.	It **will rain** again next week. Tourists **won't come** to the shops and restaurants. They**'ll stay** home.
2. Use *probably* with *will*. *Probably* comes between *will* and the main verb. In a negative sentence, *probably* comes before *won't*.	Business **will probably be** slow all week. I **probably won't make** enough money.
3. Use *if*-clauses to talk about possible results in the future. In the main clause, use *will* + base form. In the *if*-clause, use simple present. The *if*-clause can come before or after the main clause. When it comes first, use a comma between the clauses.	If the rain **continues**, we**'ll have** a lot of problems. ⎵*if*-clause⎵ ⎵main clause⎵ We**'ll have** a lot of problems if the rain **continues**. ⎵main clause⎵ ⎵*if*-clause⎵

B *Complete the sentences using the words in parentheses. Use contractions of **will** where possible.*

1. If it ____rains____ a lot this summer, fewer tourists ____will visit____. Businesses
   (rain)   (visit)

   ____probably won't make____ enough money. Some shops ____will probably close____.
   (probably / not / make)   (probably / close)

2. If housing _____ more expensive, many families _____ afford a house on
   (get)   (not / be able to)

   Cape Cod. Some families _____, and others renting _____ renting.
   (probably / move away)   (continue)

ABOVE MATERIAL FROM: NORTHSTAR LEVEL 3, THIRD EDITION

3. I heard that another seafood restaurant _____ in town. If it _____, there
　(probably / open)　　　　　　　　　　　　　　　　　　　　　(open)

_____ more jobs for the locals. But the other restaurants in town _____
　(be)　　　　　　　　　　　　　　　　　　　　　　　　　　　　　(probably / lose)

customers.

4. Traffic _____ worse if more tourists _____ their cars to Cape Cod. There
　　　　　　(get)　　　　　　　　　　　　　　　　　(bring)

_____ enough parking spaces at the beach.
　(probably / not / be)

C *Work with a partner. Read about the people who live and vacation on Cape Cod.*

CAPE COD PORTRAITS

Joe . . .
- owns Joe's Seafood Shack.
- serves 100 pounds of seafood each day.
- employs five cooks and four waitresses.

Sandy . . .
- is a high school student.
- works in a local souvenir shop during the summer.
- saves money to go to college.

Bill & Maureen . . .
- own the Cape Art Gallery.
- sell paintings and jewelry from local artists.
- employ two sales clerks.

The Harvey family . . .
- vacations on Cape Cod every summer.
- rents a house from a local.
- enjoys the area because the beaches aren't crowded.

Take turns making predictions about the future. What will happen to these people if tourism increases on Cape Cod? What will happen if tourism decreases?

EXAMPLE
STUDENT A: What **will happen** to Joe if tourism increases?
STUDENT B: If tourism **increases**, Joe's restaurant **will probably get** busier.
STUDENT A: You're right. He**'ll serve** more seafood every day. He**'ll probably need** to hire more cooks and waitresses. . . .

D *Complete the sentences with the words in parentheses.*

1. If Ali *(be)* _____**is**_____ in class tomorrow, I *(ask)* **am going to / will ask** him to join us for coffee after class.

2. If the weather *(be)* _____ nice tomorrow, I *(go)* _____ to Central Park with my friends.

3. I *(stay, not)* _____ home tomorrow if the weather *(be)* _____ nice.

4. If I *(feel, not)* _____ well tomorrow, I *(go, not)* _____ to work.

5. Masako *(stay)* _____ in bed tomorrow if she *(feel, not)* _____ well.

6. I *(stay)* _____ with my aunt and uncle if I *(go)* _____ to Miami next week.

7. If my friends *(be)* _____ busy tomorrow, I *(go)* _____ to a movie by myself.

8. If we *(continue)* _____ to pollute the land and oceans with poisons and waste, future

   generations *(suffer)* _____ .

E PAIR WORK

Work with a partner. Ask and answer questions.
PARTNER A: Ask a question that begins with **What are you going to do . . .?** Your book is open.
PARTNER B: Answer the question. Include the *if*-clause in your answer. Your book is closed.

EXAMPLE: . . . if the weather is nice tomorrow?
PARTNER A *(book open):* What are you going to do if the weather is nice tomorrow?
PARTNER B *(book closed):* If the weather is nice tomorrow, I'm going to sit outside in the sun. OR I'm going to sit outside in the sun if the weather is nice tomorrow.

1. . . . if the weather is cold tomorrow?

2. . . . if the weather is hot tomorrow?

3. . . . if you don't understand a question that I ask you?

4. . . . if class is canceled tomorrow?

ABOVE MATERIAL FROM: **BASIC ENGLISH GRAMMAR, THIRD EDITION**

5. . . . if you don't feel well tomorrow?

6. . . . if you go to *(name of a place in this city)* tomorrow?

Switch roles.
PARTNER A: Close your book.
PARTNER B: Open your book. Your turn now.

7. . . . if it rains tonight?

8. . . . if you're hungry after class today?

9. . . . if you go to *(name of a place in this city)* tomorrow?

10. . . . if you don't study tonight?

11. . . . if you lose your grammar book?

12. . . . if someone steals your *(name of a thing: bicycle, wallet, etc.)*?

F 🎧 Listen to the questions. Write your answers in complete sentences.

1. _____ .

2. _____ .

3. _____ .

4. _____ .

ABOVE MATERIAL FROM: BASIC ENGLISH GRAMMAR, THIRD EDITION

GRAMMAR

Present factual conditionals: usage

Use the present factual conditional to express general and scientific facts. Use the simple present tense or the present tense of <u>be</u> in both clauses.
> If it **rains**, flights **are** late. [fact]
> If you **heat** water to 100 degrees, it **boils**. [scientific fact]

In present factual conditional sentences, <u>when</u> (or <u>whenever</u>) is often used instead of <u>if</u>.
> **When** (or **Whenever**) it rains, flights are late.
> **When** you heat water to 100 degrees, it boils.

A *On a separate sheet of paper, write present factual conditional sentences.*

1. Water (freeze) when you (lower) its temperature below zero degrees.

2. Whenever my daughter (take) her umbrella to school, she (forget) to bring it home.

ABOVE MATERIAL FROM: TOP NOTCH 2, SECOND EDITION

3. She (go) on vacation every August if she (not have) too much work.

4. He (run) in the park if the weather (be) dry.

5. In my company, if cashiers (make) a mistake, they have to (repay) the money.

Future factual conditionals: usage and common errors

Use the future factual conditional to express what you believe will happen in the future under certain conditions or as a result of certain actions. Use the simple present tense or the present of <u>be</u> in the <u>if</u>- clause. Use a future form (<u>will</u> or <u>be going to</u>) in the result clause.

If I **go** to sleep too late tonight, I **won't be able to** get up on time, (future condition, future result)

If she **comes** home after 8:00, **I'm not going to make** dinner, (future condition, future result)

Be careful! Don't use a future form in the <u>if</u>- clause.

If I see him, I'll tell him.
NOT If I ~~will~~ see him, I'll tell him.
NOT If ~~I'm going to~~ see him, I'll tell him.

B *Circle the correct form to complete each future factual conditional sentence.*

1. If they (like / will like) the movie, they (see / will see) it again.

2. I ('m going to talk / talk) to her if she (does / 's going to do) that again.

3. If you (buy / are going to buy) some eggs, I (make / 'll make) you an omelet tonight.

4. If they (see / will see) her tomorrow, they (drive / 'll drive) her home.

5. (Are you going to study / Do you study) Italian if they (offer / will offer) it next year?

ABOVE MATERIAL FROM: TOP NOTCH 2, SECOND EDITION

Exercise Booster

A USING CAUSATIVE VERBS: MAKE, HAVE, GET

Complete the sentences with the correct form of the verbs in parentheses.

1. The general made the soldiers (*stand*) _____ at attention.

2. Don't get rid of those shoes just because they are old. Have them (*fix*) _____ at the shoe repair shop.

3. Exercise makes your heart (*beat*) _____ faster.

4. What can we do to get Marissa (*stop*) _____ smoking?

5. Jean finally got her son (*clean*) _____ his room.

6. Paula's new haircut makes her (*look*) _____ ten years younger.

7. I'm sorry, sir. Your prescription is not renewable. Have your physician (*call*) _____ us here at the pharmacy, and then we can refill it for you.

8. Please take this document to the copy store and have 15 copies (*make*) _____. There are 150 pages, so you'd better have spiral bindings (*put*) _____ on too.

B Using Causative Verbs: Make, Have, Get

Circle the letter of the correct completions. More than one completion may be correct.

1. You can _____ the bookstore order some books for you.
   a. make   **b.** have   **c.** get

2. You can order your books from the online bookstore and _____ them sent to you.
   a. make   **b.** have   **c.** get

3. If you're nice to James, maybe you can _____ him to drive you to the airport.
   a. make   **b.** have   **c.** get

4. I'll _____ the taxi driver take me to the airport.
   a. make   **b.** have   **c.** get

5. The comedian is so funny. I can't help laughing even though I'm sad. That comedian can _____ anyone laugh.
   a. make   **b.** have   **c.** get

6. The students tried to _____ the professor to postpone the exam, but he didn't.
   a. make   **b.** have   **c.** get

7. I'm going to _____ my car washed on Saturday.
   a. make   **b.** have   **c.** get

8. Ms. Andrews isn't there? _____ her call me, please.
   a. Make   **b.** Have   **c.** Get

9. A magician can _____ a rabbit appear and disappear.
   a. make   **b.** have   **c.** get

C Expressing Past Habit: Used to

*Complete the sentences. Use **used to** and the given information.*

1. When James was young, he hated school. Now he likes it.

   James _____ **used to hate school** _____, but now he likes it.

2. Ann was a secretary for many years, but now she owns her own business.

   Ann _____, but now she owns her own business.

3. Before Adam got married, he played tennis five times a week.

   Adam _____ five times a week.

4. When we raised our own chickens, we had fresh eggs every morning.

   We _____ every morning when we raised our own chickens.

ABOVE MATERIAL FROM: UNDERSTANDING AND USING ENGLISH GRAMMAR, 4TH ED WORKBOOK

5. When Ben was a child, he often crawled under his bed and put his hands over his ears when he heard thunder.

Ben _____ and _____ when he heard thunder.

6. When I lived in my home town, I went to the beach every weekend. Now I don't go to the beach every weekend.

I _____ to the beach every weekend, but now I don't.

7. Joshua has a new job. He has to wear a suit every day. When he was a student, he always wore jeans.

Joshua _____ jeans every day, but now he has to wear a suit.

8. In the past, Sara hated pets. But now she has two cats, and she likes them very much.

Sara _____ pets, but now she likes them a lot.

9. When I was young, I ate peanuts. Now I am allergic to them.

I _____ peanuts, but now I am allergic to them.

D As . . . As

*Make comparisons using **as . . . as**.*

1. Rita is very busy. Jason is very busy.

→ Rita is ___*(just) as busy as Jason (is)*_____.

2. Rita is not very busy at all. Jason is very, very busy.

→ Rita isn't ___*(nearly) as busy as Jason (is)*_____.

3. I was tired. Susan was very tired.

→ I wasn't _____.

4. Adam wasn't tired at all. Susan was very tired.

→ Adam wasn't _____.

5. Anne is lazy. Her sister Amanda is equally lazy.

→ Anne is _____.

6. Their brother Alan is extremely lazy.

→ Anne and Amanda are lazy, but they are not _____.

E As...As

*Make comparisons using **as...as** and the adjective in parentheses. Use **not** as necessary.*

1. Adults have more strength than children, (*strong*)

   → Children _____**aren't as strong as**_____ adults.

2. Tom and Jerry are the same height. (*tall*)

   → Tom _____ Jerry.

3. Dr. Green has a little money. Dr. Brown has a lot of money. (*wealthy*)

   → Dr. Green _____ Dr. Brown.

4. City air is often polluted. Country air is often fresh and clear. (*polluted*)

   → Country air _____ city air.

5. Paula studies a little bit. Jack studies a lot. (*studious*)

   → Paula _____ Jack.

6. Math courses are easy for me, but language courses aren't. (*difficult*)

   → Math courses _____ language courses for me.

F As...As

Part I. Complete each expression with the correct phrase.

as a bat	as a mouse	as a pillow
as a bird	as a picture	✓ as snow
as a bone	as pie	as a wink
as ice		

1. very white: as white _____**as snow**_____.

2. very cold: as cold _____.

3. very pretty: as pretty _____.

4. can't see anything: as blind _____.

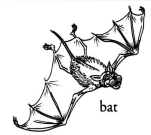

bat

ABOVE MATERIAL FROM: FUNDAMENTALS OF ENGLISH GRAMMAR, 4TH ED WORKBOOK

5. very dry: as dry _____.

6. very soft: as soft _____

7. very quick: as quick _____.

8. very quiet: as quiet _____.

9. very free: as free _____.

10. very easy: as easy _____.

pie

wink

G Expressing Ability and Possibility

Choose the correct completion.

1. **A:** Are you running in the big race tomorrow, Alan?

   B: No, I'm not. I _____ run. I broke my foot on Saturday and now it's in a cast.
   - a. can
   - b. can't
   - c. may
   - d. may not

2. **A:** Where's Tracy? I've been looking for her all morning.

   B: I haven't seen her. She _____ be sick.
   - a. can
   - b. can't
   - c. might
   - d. might not

3. **A:** I heard that Jessica has gotten a scholarship to Duke University!

   B: It's not definite yet, but she _____ get one. The admissions office says that it's possible and they will let us know next month.
   - a. can
   - b. can't
   - c. might
   - d. might not

4. **A:** Larry has been in New York for a couple of months. Is he going to stay there or return home?

   B: It depends. If he _____ find a job there soon, he'll stay. If not, he'll come home.
   - a. can
   - b. can't
   - c. may
   - d. may not

5. **A:** Is Jodie a doctor now?

   B: Not yet, but almost. She finished medical school last month, but she hasn't taken her exams yet. She _____ be a doctor until she passes them.
   - a. can
   - b. can't
   - c. might
   - d. might not

6. **A:** When are you going to sell your old car?

   B: As soon as I _____ find someone to buy it!
   - a. can
   - b. can't
   - c. may
   - d. may not

H POLITE QUESTIONS: MAY I, COULD I, CAN I

Complete the conversations. Write the letter of the question that matches each answer.

> **a.** Can I borrow the book when you finish it?
> **b.** Could I pick you up at 6:30 instead of 6:00?
> **c.** Could we watch the comedy instead of the war movie?
> **d.** May I ask you a question?
> **e.** May I have some more potatoes, please?
> **f.** May I help you?

1. **A:** _____
   B: Yes. They're delicious, aren't they?

2. **A:** _____
   B: Yes. What would you like to know?

3. **A:** _____
   B: Thanks. I want to buy this.

4. **A:** _____
   B: That's a little late.

5. **A:** _____
   B: Sure. I'm in the mood for something funny.

6. **A:** _____
   B: Yes. I'll probably finish it tonight.

ABOVE MATERIAL FROM: FUNDAMENTALS OF ENGLISH GRAMMAR, 4TH ED WORKBOOK

PREPOSITION + GERUND

a. Kate *insisted **on coming*** with us. **b.** We're *excited **about going*** to Tahiti. **c.** I *apologized **for being*** late.	A preposition is followed by a gerund, not an infinitive. In (a): The preposition (*on*) is followed by a gerund (*coming*).

Common Expressions with Prepositions Followed by Gerunds

be afraid **of** (doing something)	be good **at**	be responsible **for**
apologize **for**	insist **on**	stop (someone) **from**
believe **in**	instead **of**	thank (someone) **for**
dream **about/of**	be interested **in**	be tired **of**
be excited **about**	look forward **to**	worry **about**/be worried **about**
feel **like**	be nervous **about**	
forgive (someone) **for**	plan **on**	

ABOVE MATERIAL FROM: FUNDAMENTALS OF ENGLISH GRAMMAR, FOURTH EDITION

1 LOOKING AT GRAMMAR

Complete the sentences with a preposition + gerund *and the given words.*

1. I'm looking forward   +   go away for the weekend

   → I'm looking forward **to** going away for the weekend.

2. Thank you   +   hold the door open

3. I'm worried   +   be late for my appointment

4. Are you interested   +   go to the beach with us

5. I apologized   +   be late

6. Are you afraid   +   fly in small planes

7. Are you nervous   +   take your driver's test

8. We're excited   +   see the soccer game

9. Tariq insisted   +   pay the restaurant bill

10. Eva dreams   +   become a veterinarian someday

11. I don't feel   +   eat right now

12. Please forgive me   +   not write sooner

13. I'm tired   +   live with five roommates

14. I believe   +   be honest at all times

15. Let's plan   +   meet at the restaurant at six

16. Who's responsible   +   clean the classroom

17. The police stopped us +   enter the building

18. Jake's not very good +   cut his own hair

ABOVE MATERIAL FROM: FUNDAMENTALS OF ENGLISH GRAMMAR, FOURTH EDITION

PRACTICE

Test yourself and practice the preposition combinations. Follow these steps:

1. **Cover** the ANSWERS column with a piece of paper.

2. Complete the SENTENCES.

3. Then remove the paper and check your answers.

4. Then **cover** both the ANSWERS and the SENTENCES to complete your own REFERENCE LIST.

5. Again check your answers.

PREPOSITION COMBINATIONS

Answers	Sentences	Reference List
from	He was absent _____**from**_____ work.	**be absent** _____**from**_____ s.t.**
of	I'm afraid _____**of**_____ rats.	**be afraid** _____**of**_____ s.t./s.o.**
about	I'm angry _____**about**_____ it.	**be angry** _____ s.t.
at / with	I'm angry _____ you.	**be angry** _____ s.o.
about	I'm curious _____ many things.	**be curious** _____ s.t./s.o.
to	This is equal _____ that.	**be equal** _____ s.t./s.o.
with	I'm familiar _____ that book.	**be familiar** _____ s.t./s.o.
of	The room is full _____ people.	**be full** _____ (people/things)
for	I'm happy _____ you.	**be happy** _____ s.o.
about	I'm happy _____ your good luck.	**be happy** _____ s.t.
to	He's kind _____ people and animals.	**be kind** _____ s.o.
to	She's always nice _____ me.	**be nice** _____ s.o.
to	Are you polite _____ strangers?	**be polite** _____ s.o.
for	I'm ready _____ my trip.	**be ready** _____ s.t.
for	She's thirsty _____ lemonade.	**be thirsty** _____ s.t.

**s.t. = "something"; s.o. = "someone"

J PREPOSITION + GERUND

Complete the sentences. Use prepositions and gerunds.

1. Bill interrupted me. He apologized _____**for**_____ that.

   Bill apologized __**for interrupting**__ me.

2. I like to learn about other countries and cultures. I'm interested _____ that.

   I'm interested _____ about other countries and cultures.

3. I helped Ann. She thanked me _____ that.

   Ann thanked me _____ her.

4. Nadia wanted to walk to work. She insisted _____ that.

   We offered Nadia a ride, but she insisted _____ to work.

5. Nick lost my car keys. I forgave him _____ that.

   I forgave Nick _____ my car keys when he borrowed my car.

6. Sara wants to go out to eat just because she feels _____ it.

   She feels _____ out to eat.

 ABOVE MATERIAL FROM: FUNDAMENTALS OF ENGLISH GRAMMAR, 4TH ED WORKBOOK

7. I'm not a good artist. I try to draw faces, but I'm not very good _____ it.

   I'm not good _____ faces.

8. Mr. and Mrs. Reed have been saving some money for their retirement. They believe _____ that.

   Mr. and Mrs. Reed believe _____ money for their retirement.

9. I may forget the words I'm supposed to say in my graduation speech. I'm worried _____ that. I'm worried _____ the words in my speech.

10. The children are going to go to Disneyland. They're excited _____ that.

    The children are excited _____ to Disneyland.

11. Their parents are going to Disneyland too. They are looking forward _____ that.

    Their parents are looking forward _____ there too.

12. Max doesn't like to stay in hotels because he is scared of heights. He is afraid _____ that.

    Max is afraid _____ in hotels.

K VERB + GERUND OR INFINITIVE

Choose the correct completion.

1. I would like (*inviting* / *to invite*) you and some of my other friends for dinner sometime.

2. I enjoyed (*being* / *to be*) with my family at the lake last summer.

3. My parents can't afford (*paying* / *to pay*) all of my college expenses.

4. Theresa, would you mind (*mailing* / *to mail*) this letter on your way home?

5. Do you expect (*passing* / *to pass*) this course? If so, you'd better work harder.

6. Mr. Reed refused (*considering* / *to consider*) my proposal. He had already made up his mind.

7. I wish he would consider (*accepting* / *to accept*) my proposal. I know I can do the job.

8. I don't think I'll ever finish (*reading* / *to read*) this report. It just goes on and on.

ABOVE MATERIAL FROM: FUNDAMENTALS OF ENGLISH GRAMMAR, 4TH ED WORKBOOK

L CLAUSES WITH IF

Directions: Complete the sentences with the correct verbs in parentheses.

1. If Ellen (*wins, will win*) _____ **wins** _____ a scholarship, she (*attends, will attend*)

   _____ a four-year college or university.

2. If she (*goes, will go*) _____ to a college or university, she (*is going to study, studies*)

   _____ chemistry.

3. If she (enjoys, will enjoy) _____ chemistry, she (takes, will take) _____ pre-med* courses.

4. She (applies, will apply) _____ to medical school if she (is going to do, does) _____ well in her pre-med courses.

5. If she (will attend, attends) _____ medical school, she (majors in, is going to major in) _____ family medicine.

6. If she (completes, is going to complete) _____ her training, she (works, is going to work) _____ around the world helping people.

M CLAUSES WITH IF

Directions: Complete the sentences with the verbs in parentheses.

1. If it (be) _____**is**_____ sunny tomorrow, Jake (work) ___**is going to work**___ OR _____**will work**_____ outside in his garden.

2. If it (rain) _____ tomorrow, I (work, not) _____ in my garden.

3. If Beth (get) _____ a high score on her college entrance exams, her parents (be) _____ proud of her.

4. Her parents (get) _____ her extra help if she (do, not) _____ well.

5. If Mark (get) _____ a job as a tour guide this summer, he (earn) _____ enough money for school next year.

6. If Mark (get, not) _____ a good job, he (delay) _____ school for a year.

7. If Lesley (feel) _____ sick tomorrow, she (come, not) _____ to school.

8. She (call) _____ you for the homework assignments if she (miss) _____ class.

9. If Brian (need) _____ help this weekend, we (help) _____ him.

10. We (make) _____ other plans if he (need, not) _____ help next week.

N BEFORE, AFTER, AND IF

Directions: Complete the sentences with the words in parentheses.

On Ana's birthday, Alex is going to ask Ana to marry him.

He (ask) ___**is going to ask / will ask**___ her after they (celebrate)
              1
___**celebrate**___ her birthday at a restaurant. Before Alex
          2

pre-med = classes that prepare a student for medical school.

ABOVE MATERIAL FROM: BASIC ENGLISH GRAMMAR, THIRD EDITION WORKBOOK

(talk) _____ to Ana, he *(meet)* _____ with
                3   4

her parents.

If they *(agree)* _____, Alex *(buy)* _____ an
                5   6

engagement ring for Ana. If Ana *(say)* _____ "yes," Alex
                                    7

(give) _____ it to her for her present. If Ana
                8

(say, not) _____ "yes," Alex *(keep)* _____ the
                9   10

ring and try again later.

O HABITUAL PRESENT

Directions: Make sentences using the habitual present.

PART I. Match each phrase in Column A with a phrase in Column B. Write the letter in the blank.

COLUMN A	COLUMN B
1. __F__ drink too much coffee	**A.** my eyes get red
2. _____ cry	**B.** get home late
3. _____ not pay my electric bill	**C.** not answer it
4. _____ the phone rings in the middle of the night	**D.** get low grades on the tests
5. _____ get to work late	**E.** have no electricity
6. _____ have a big breakfast	✓**F.** feel shaky and nervous
7. _____ not do my homework	**G.** have a lot of energy

Important Words and Phrases

VOCABULARY WORD	DEFINITION

UNIT 1–Getting Things Done

give (me) a ride _____

keep an eye on (my things) _____

lend _____

fill in for _____

pick up (a sandwich) _____

understand _____

no problem _____

don't worry about it _____

run late for an appointment _____

have a meeting in an hour _____

expect an important call _____

dry-clean a suit/dress/sweater _____

repair shoes _____

frame a picture/photo/
painting/drawing/diploma _____

deliver a package _____

shorten/lengthen a skirt/
dress/pants _____

print a sign _____

copy a report _____

someone is coming to visit _____

going on a vacation/
business trip _____

VOCABULARY WORD	DEFINITION

there's going to be a
party/meeting _____

I owe you one _____

thanks a million _____

you're a lifesaver _____

I know this is last minute _____

I won't keep you any longer _____

lengthen eyelashes _____

color eyebrows _____

straighten/whiten teeth _____

shorten nose _____

plump lips _____

color/lengthen/style/curl/
straighten/braid hair _____

whiten/tan/tattoo/paint skin _____

paint nails/hands/soles of feet _____

UNIT 2–Eating Well

calcium _____

carbohydrates _____

protein _____

fats _____

oils _____

VOCABULARY WORD	DEFINITION	VOCABULARY WORD	DEFINITION
sweets		take care of it	
dairy		it couldn't hurt	
meat		I'll just be a second	
fish		run anti-virus software	
beans		try rebooting	
fruit		contact a technical expert	
vegetables		check if it's turned on	
bread		buy a new computer	
grains		that sometimes works	
pasta		that might help	
rarely		that may do the trick	
1–5 servings a day		a pull-down menu	
at most meals		the tool bar	
I couldn't resist		the scroll bar	
I have to admit		open a file	
I have no idea		save a file	
I'd better pass		print a file	
I'm watching my weight		cut text	
just a bite		copy text	
The High-Fiber Diet		paste text	
The Vegan Diet		select/highlight text	
The Atkins Diet		the cursor	
The Low-Fat Diet		scroll up/down	
crazy about/not crazy about		click on an icon	
a big (meat) eater		attach (a file)	
a big (coffee) drinker		upload (a file)	
a (chocolate) addict		download (a file)	
a (pizza) lover		surf the internet	
can't stand		join (an online group)	
don't care for		post (a message)	
not much of a (pizza) eater		I was wondering if you might	
not much of a (coffee) drinker		be able to recommend	
sushi			
mangoes			

UNIT 4—Health Matters

VOCABULARY WORD	DEFINITION
(thanks for) fitting me in	
(this tooth) is killing me	
(it's been) bothering me	
let's have a look	
see what's going on	
dizzy	
nauseous	
weak	
short of breath	
vomit	
cough	
sneeze	

VOCABULARY WORD	DEFINITION
pasta	
ice cream	
asparagus	

UNIT 3—Living with Computers

VOCABULARY WORD	DEFINITION
a monitor	
a keyboard	
a mouse	
a touchpad	
fool around	
nothing happens	

VOCABULARY WORD	DEFINITION	VOCABULARY WORD	DEFINITION
wheeze	_____	exciting	_____
in my chest	_____	boring	_____
in my hip	_____	depressing	_____
in my ribs	_____	annoying	_____
in my stomach	_____	scary	_____
cough medicine	_____	on weekends	_____
an antibiotic	_____	on vacations	_____
an antacid	_____	with your friends and family	_____
an ointment	_____	for lunch/dinner	_____
vitamins	_____		
tomorrow	_____		

UNIT 6–Culture and Commerce

VOCABULARY WORD	DEFINITION	VOCABULARY WORD	DEFINITION
(early) next week	_____	afford	_____
At the end of the week	_____	controversy	_____
the week of	_____	depend on	_____
are you (coughing)?	_____	degrading	_____
did you try. . . .	_____	make a living	_____
you should/you better	_____	preserve	_____
why don't you try. . . ?	_____	season	_____
How about. . . ?	_____	souvenir	_____
you must feel awful/terrible	_____	stretch	_____
that must hurt	_____	tourist attraction	_____
a painkiller	_____	tradition	_____
cold tablets	_____	village	_____
a nasal spray/a decongestant	_____	wrap	_____
eye drops	_____	get off the beaten path	_____
an antihistamine	_____	locals	_____
		impact	_____
		in the long run	_____

UNIT 5–About Personality

VOCABULARY WORD	DEFINITION
relaxing	_____
enjoyable	_____

way of life _____

find a compromise _____